# THE FABLES OF
# ÆSOP

# THE FABLES OF
# ÆSOP

## *112 Moral Tales Retold*

SELECTED AND EDITED BY RUTH SPRIGGS

*With an Introduction by Anne Wood*

ILLUSTRATED BY FRANK BABER

RAND McNALLY & COMPANY
Chicago    New York    San Francisco

# Contents

ISBN 0-528-82070-2

Printed in the United States of America
by Rand McNally & Company

Library of Congress Catalog Card Number: 75-41965

# Introduction

I believe this edition of Aesop's Fables will find its way to countless family bookshelves, not because it is a classic but because it is fun, good reading and good value. I enjoyed it very much and so did my children aged ten and six, for this is one of the few books that can be confidently recommended over a very wide age range.

It has been prepared with the utmost care and is just right for that stage when the reading scheme has been left behind but children seem reluctant to go on to long continuous "reads".

Not that Aesop all those centuries ago would have known about reading problems! According to tradition he was a Greek slave, living in the sixth century BC. His stories were to be told; cleverly presenting human problems through the dilemmas of animal characters, a tradition that can be traced in the cultures of many different races. Though they were first told so long ago, the stories are as relevant today as ever. Even now children hang on to the "moral" as they would to the solution of a difficult puzzle.

Individual fables have been illustrated over the years by renowned artists but the pictures in this book have been made with children's known tastes in mind and are full of storybook detail in traditional style. It is a great pleasure to be able to recommend a book for content and quality of production and for child appeal but most of all for a sense of fun.

Maybe Aesop all those years ago was observing the irony of man's existence but he must have had a sense of humour too. This above all is captured here and is the additional quality that combines with all the rest to make this version of Aesop's Fables special.

Anne Wood
Editor, *Books for Your Children*

# The Lion and the Mouse

A LION was sleeping in his lair one hot afternoon when a mouse ran over his nose and woke him up. The lion snarled and was just about to crush the mouse with his huge paw when:

"Oh spare me, my lord," cried the mouse. "I am really not worth killing. I mean you no harm – and I don't even taste nice."

The lion snarled sleepily.

"Besides," the mouse squeaked, "perhaps I can do something for you one day if you spare me now."

The lion gave a great roar of laughter but he lifted his paw and the mouse skipped out of reach. Still laughing, the lion sank back to his dreams.

Not long after, the lion was hunting in the woods when he fell into a trap. Some hunters had stretched a trip rope across one of his favourite paths. They had suspended a huge net above the path and had fixed it so that when the lion fell over the rope, the net would fall down and cover him, holding him prisoner until morning.

The lion twisted and turned and scratched and bit, but the more he struggled the more tightly he seemed to be held in the net. Soon he could not move at all. With no hope of escape, he began to roar and his mighty voice echoed through every corner of the forest.

Now it happened that the mouse was also out hunting that night. Of course he quickly recognized the lion's voice and he ran as fast as he could to the spot. He saw at a glance what the situation was and pausing only to say "Don't worry, sir, I'll have you out in no time," and "Keep still, sir, *please*," he began to gnaw and nibble the thick cords of the net. In a very short time the lion's front paws were free; then his head and mane; then his back legs and finally his tail.

The little mouse had done something for the great lion, just as he had promised.

In fact, he had saved his life.

*Do not judge people's usefulness by their appearance.*

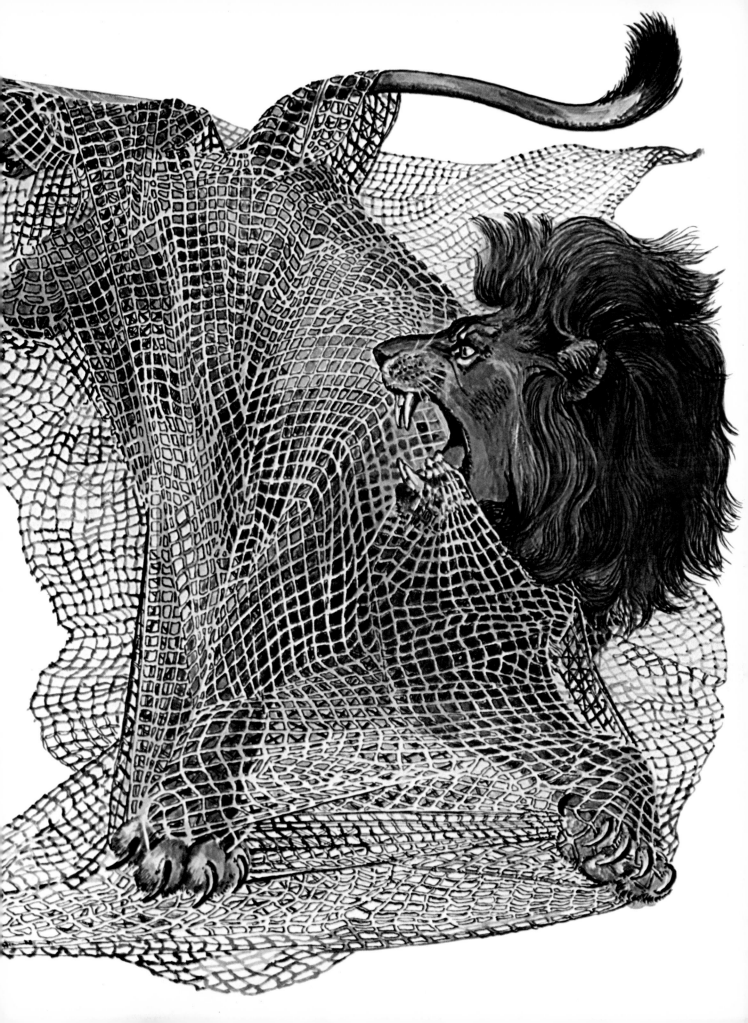

## The Donkey and the Salt

THERE was once a merchant who kept a donkey. They travelled all over the countryside, buying and selling different kinds of things. Sometimes the merchant would sell cloth and beads. At other times he would sell fruit and fresh green vegetables. In fact he would sell anything if he could make a bit of money out of it.

One day he heard that salt was being sold cheaply at the seaside.

"I can get a fine price for that in the villages in the mountains," he thought and he set off with his donkey to buy some.

The salt was certainly very cheap so the merchant bought a good supply and loaded it on the donkey's back. All went well until they came to a narrow rocky pass in the mountains with a deep stream flowing through it. The merchant was leading the donkey carefully along a slippery ledge when suddenly the donkey lost his footing and slipped heavily into the stream.

As the donkey struggled to swim against the current the water melted the salt he was carrying and washed it away, leaving only the empty bags fixed to the saddle. With no weight to pull him down the donkey easily reached the bank and continued cheerfully on his way.

Soon afterwards the merchant decided to buy another load of salt. Once more he took his donkey to the seaside, loaded him up and set off for the mountains. As soon as they came to the narrow rocky pass the donkey remembered how easily he had lost his heavy load and how pleasant it had been travelling without it. This time he slipped into the stream on purpose and stayed there struggling in the water until the salt had quite melted away.

The merchant was not at all pleased. He had lost two good loads of salt and he suspected that the donkey had played a trick on him. He thought of a way to play a trick on the donkey in return.

The next time he went to the seaside he bought a great load of sponges. The donkey set off happily.

"These bags are light," he thought, "and by the time I get to the pass they will be lighter still."

Before long they came to the rocky ledge. Once more the donkey rolled himself into the water and lay struggling, waiting for the load to melt away as it had done twice before.

Instead of melting away, however, the sponges quickly soaked up the water.

"What's this?" thought the donkey as he felt the bags getting heavier and heavier on his back.

"Something is wrong here." Then as he felt himself sinking lower and lower in the stream: "Help, master, help!"

The merchant leaned over and pulled him gasping and spluttering out of the water.

"We'll go home now, shall we?" said the merchant. And he led the dripping donkey on up the mountainside.

"With double the load I started with," thought the donkey sadly as he plodded along towards the village.

*Every problem has a different solution.*

## The Lark

A FAMILY of larks once lived in a field of ripening corn. Every day when she went to look for food, the mother told her chicks:

"Listen carefully to everything you hear. One day soon the reapers will come to cut the corn, and we must find another home before that happens."

One day while she was away the farmer came to examine the corn.

"It is time to get my neighbours together to cut the corn," he said to his son.

The little larks listened carefully and told their mother what he had said.

"Let's go at once," they cried. "The reapers will be here in the morning and we shall not be able to escape."

"There is plenty of time yet," said the mother lark calmly. "If he is relying on his neighbours he will have to wait some time before he gets the corn in."

The next day the farmer came again. The sun was hotter than ever, and the corn was riper but nothing had been done to harvest it.

"There is no time to lose," he said. "It is no use depending on the neighbours. I must get all my relations to help." He turned to his son. "Go and call your uncles and cousins and make sure that they begin tomorrow without fail."

The little larks were very frightened and again they begged their mother to take them away at once.

"If that is all he said there is nothing to worry about. His relations have harvesting of their own to do. He won't get them to do his work for a while yet. But tomorrow listen carefully. I want to know every word he says."

The next day the farmer came as usual to inspect the grain. Now the corn was so ripe that it was beginning to fall to the ground, but still no one had come to cut it.

"We cannot wait for our neighbours and relations a day longer," said the farmer. "Go and hire some men and we will start work tomorrow ourselves."

"Take us away, take us away," said the little larks as soon as their mother returned. "They are going to cut the corn tomorrow."

"What exactly did they say?" asked the mother. "Did they say they would cut the corn themselves?"

"Yes, yes," squeaked the larks. "They are coming to cut the corn themselves."

"It really is time to go then," said the mother. "If a man decides to do something himself instead of leaving it to other people, then he means to get it done. Come, try out your wings. We must fly to the next meadow."

*If you want something done, do it yourself.*

## The Leopard and the Fox

A LEOPARD and a fox were arguing about which of them was the better animal.

"My spotted coat is the most beautiful fur in the world," said the leopard.

"You cannot see my beauty," said the fox, "for it is inside my head. But it is better to be wise than beautiful in this forest, my friend."

*Cleverness is more useful than beauty.*

# The Goose that laid the Golden Eggs

A FARMER and his wife once had a goose that laid a solid gold egg every day. Each evening they settled it securely in its pen in the corner of their kitchen with a bowl of the best corn and a saucer of fresh water. Each morning they found a new, bright yellow egg in its nest of sweet hay.

One day the farmer's wife said to her husband: "These eggs are all very well, my dear, but though I suppose we will be rich in the end, it is a very slow way of making a fortune. By the time we get it, it will not be worth half what it is today. Now I have an idea. It is obvious to me that there must be a great store of golden eggs inside our goose. Why should we wait all our lives for her to lay them? Go and get the knife and we'll have all the gold now while we can still enjoy it."

"Well," said the farmer doubtfully, "it seems a sad way to treat a good bird. But on the other hand . . ."

Without another word he killed the goose and cut her open – only to find that inside she was just like any other goose, with no sign of a golden egg at all.

"We'll not get rich quickly or slowly now, my dear," said the farmer sadly.

*Don't be greedy.*

## The Hare and the Hound

ONE day a dog found a hare hiding under a bush. The hare streaked off across the fields with the dog bounding along behind. The dog was not fast enough, however, and he soon gave up the chase.

A man working in the field watched the whole thing and as the dog came trotting past he said:

"Fancy letting a little animal like that outrun you. He was going twice as fast as you were. You must be getting old."

"You forget why we were running," answered the dog calmly. "There's a big difference between running for your dinner and running for your life."

## The Lion in Love

ONCE upon a time a lion fell in love with a woodcutter's daughter and asked her father for her hand in marriage.

The woodcutter was not at all pleased at the thought of having a lion for his son-in-law and at first he refused even to talk about it. The lion looked so angry, however, that the poor woodcutter was afraid.

"I'll have to think of something," he said to himself, "or this king of beasts will tear me to pieces, and my daughter too, I shouldn't wonder."

The woodcutter thought and thought and at last he knew what to do.

"My daughter and I have discussed your proposal very carefully," he said to the lion. "We are both very flattered that you should want to marry into our poor family. But sir, what great sharp claws you have! What strong teeth! The truth is, sir, that my daughter is a bit frightened of you – and what girl would not be? You are a very powerful, and important person you know.

"However, I think that there is something that you can do about it. If you have all your teeth drawn and your claws cut right down she will feel quite safe. Then you'll make the best husband in the world, I am sure."

The lion was really very much in love with the woodcutter's daughter so he went away at once and found someone to take his teeth out and cut his mighty claws right down. Then he came confidently back to the woodcutter's hut.

"Let me see your claws," said the woodcutter. The lion held up his soft paws.

"Good. Now your teeth." The lion opened his mouth to show his toothless gums.

"Very good," said the woodcutter. "Now that we are equals I will show you what I really think of you as a son-in-law!"

And the woodcutter took up his thick stick and drove the helpless lion back into the forest.

*A man in love is easily deceived.*

## The Boy in the River

ONE day a boy was paddling in a stream when he stumbled in a hollow and fell into a deep pool. As he could not swim, he began to shout and scream for help, waving his arms and kicking his legs as he tried to stay afloat.

Just when he was beginning to think he would drown an old man came walking past on the river bank.

"You stupid child," said the man. "You know you are not supposed to paddle in that river. How many times have you been told that it is dangerous. Your mother ought to give you a good spanking."

"Oh please," spluttered the boy as he struggled to keep his head above water, "I will listen to as many lectures, as you like, but please, please rescue me first."

*There is a time to talk and a time to act.*

## The Donkey and the Statue

A DONKEY was once chosen to carry a holy statue through the town. Crowds of people came from all over the countryside to see the procession. They lined the sides of the street, pushing and jostling to get nearer to the front.

As the donkey came past all the people bowed down to pray to the statue. Some of them reached out their hands to touch it; others fell on their knees in the road in front of it. The donkey began to feel he was a very important animal.

"Fancy all these people showing me so much respect," he thought. "I never knew I was so powerful. To think that all this time I have been doing everything my master told me."

He decided to try out his power.

"I really don't feel like walking any further," he said to himself. "I'll just stand here for a while and let the people admire me." And he refused to take another step.

Thwack! A sharp blow fell on his back.

"Get along with you," hissed his master angrily. "What do you mean by holding up the procession like this?"

"All in good time," replied the donkey grandly. "I am just giving these good people a chance to look at me."

His master began to laugh.

"You poor stupid animal," he said, pulling the donkey's mane to make him walk on. "The people are not interested in you. It is the statue on your back they are here to see. Come along now before I lose my temper."

*Make sure it's really you people are praising, before you give yourself airs.*

17

# The Parrot and the Cat

A MAN once bought a brilliantly-coloured parrot. Instead of locking it up in a cage or chaining it to a perch, he allowed it to fly free all over the house. The parrot was delighted at this and flapped from room to room, shrieking and screaming with happiness. At last he settled on the edge of a rich curtain.

"Who on earth are you?" said a cross voice from below. "Stop that terrible noise at once."

The parrot saw a cat staring up at him from the carpet.

"I'm a parrot. I've just arrived and I'm to make as much noise as I can," he said.

"Well I've lived here all my life," replied the cat. "I was born in this very house and I learned from my mother that it is best to keep quiet here."

"Keep quiet then," said the parrot cheerfully. "I don't know what you do around here, but I know my job. My master bought me for my voice and I'm going to make sure he hears it."

*Different people are valued for different things.*

## Hot and Cold

A MAN and a satyr sat down to eat together. It was a cold day and the man blew on his fingers to warm them before he picked up his knife.

"Why do you do that?" asked the satyr.

"My hands are cold," replied the man. "I blow on them to warm them up."

Soon the food arrived: two plates of steaming hot stew and vegetables. The man leaned over to blow on the meat.

"Why do you do that now?" asked the satyr. "The food is hot already."

"The food is *too* hot," said the man. "I blow on it to cool it down."

The satyr stood up.

"I'm not staying here any longer," he said. "What kind of a man is it that blows hot and cold with the same mouth?"

## The Stray Dogs

FIVE stray dogs were roaming about looking for something to eat when they came to a deep river. On the river bed they could see a bag full of bones that someone had thrown away. The bones looked very good and the dogs sat on the bank with their mouths watering, wondering how they could get at them.

"There is only one thing to do," said the oldest dog at last. "We must drink all the water. Then we shall be able to jump in and feast to our hearts' content. Come on, let's begin."

The five dogs began to lap at the water flowing past. They drank and they drank and they drank. In fact they drank so much that before long they burst themselves with drinking!

The river took no notice. It flowed on as full as ever, washing over the bones, wearing them away in its current until only a pile of whitened sticks remained.

*Don't try to do the impossible.*

## The Disobedient Donkey

THERE was once a donkey who never did what he was told. If his master wanted him to go to the right he pulled to the left. If his master wanted him to go to the left he pulled to the right. In fact he always wanted to do the exact opposite to what his master said.

It happened that one day the donkey was being driven along a twisty track up a high mountainside. All of a sudden he decided that he did not want to stay on the path and he made off as fast as he could towards the edge, where the mountain fell steeply away. The donkey was just about to fall head-first over the edge of the cliff when his master caught him by the tail.

"Come back, you stupid animal," said his master, pulling his tail and backing away up the slope towards the path. "Come this way or you will fall."

"This way, this way," said the donkey stubbornly, pulling away from the man. "I don't want to go that way."

He pulled so hard that the man was forced to let go. The man sat down with a bump on the grass – and the donkey plunged braying with triumph over the edge of the cliff.

*There is no point being stubborn just for the sake of it.*

## The Travellers and the Plane Tree

TWO men were walking along one summer day. Soon it became too hot to go any further and, seeing a large plane tree nearby, they threw themselves on the ground to rest in its shade.

Gazing up into the branches one man said to the other: "What a useless tree this is. It does not have fruit or nuts that we can eat and we cannot even use its wood for anything."

"Don't be so ungrateful," rustled the tree in reply. "I am being extremely useful to you at this very moment, shielding you from the hot sun. And you call me a good-for-nothing!"

*Everything has its use.*

## Doctor Wolf

A WOLF once chased a donkey into the corner of a field. The donkey could not run very fast because he had trodden on a sharp thorn which had stuck fast in his hoof.

"Before you kill me, Mr Wolf," said the donkey, "I wonder if you would be kind enough to take the thorn out of my foot. I am afraid that when you are eating me it may stick in your throat and choke you."

"Thanks for telling me," said the wolf. "Turn round and let me have a look."

The donkey turned obediently round and raised his foot. The wolf leaned over to take the thorn in his teeth and the donkey kicked – hard. The next moment the wolf was flying through the air like a small grey cloud. He landed flat on his back in the middle of the field.

"That serves me right," he said as he watched the donkey galloping off to safety. "After all, I'm a wolf, not a doctor. I should have stuck to what I knew. Now, what about my supper?"

## The Fox and the Hen

A FOX once crept into an outhouse and looked around for something to eat. The only thing he could see was an old hen, perched high up above his head, far out of reach.

"Good evening, hen," he said politely. "I just called to see how you were. I heard that you were not well and I just had to come to see you myself. I know a little about illness, you know. Why don't you come down and let me feel your pulse. You really don't look well."

The hen settled herself more securely on her high perch.

"You are right, fox. I am not at all well. In fact I am so ill that I cannot be disturbed. I know you will understand if I don't come down just now. I'm very afraid that if I do I shall catch my death!"

*It is good to know who your enemies are.*

21

# The Wolf and the Crane

A WOLF was eating his supper one day when a bone stuck in his throat. Choking and coughing, he howled about the countryside asking every animal he met to help him.

"There's a good reward for anyone who can save me," he spluttered.

A crane heard about this promise and offered to help.

"Open your mouth wide, wolf," she said, and poked her long beak deep into his throat. "Here is the bone that has been troubling you," she added politely as soon as her head was out of the wolf's mouth. "I trust you will now be able to give me the reward you promised."

"Reward," laughed the wolf, showing all his gleaming teeth in a mean smile and quite forgetting his sore throat. "You are lucky I did not snap your head off with one bite. That should be enough of a reward for you, ungrateful bird. And it is certainly all you will get from me."

*If you only help people because you can get something out of it for yourself, you'll be disappointed.*

## The Astronomer

THERE was once an astronomer who spent every night walking about gazing at the stars. One night he was staring at the sky as usual when he tripped over a pile of rubble and fell into a deep hole in the road.

A friend of his happened to be passing and, hearing his cries for help, went over to pull him out.

"The trouble with you," he said as he dusted him down, "is that you spend so much time thinking about the mysteries of the universe that you quite forget the ordinary troubles of everyday life. If you refuse to learn the ways of this world, you must expect to come to grief."

## The Lion, the Cock and the Elephant

"I'M NOT fit to be king of the beasts," groaned the lion to the elephant one day. "Here I am, a great strong animal with teeth that can rip you apart and yet I am afraid of a common or garden cock. I have only to hear one crowing in the distance and all my strength and courage disappear."

The lion looked up, full of self-pity. All this time the elephant had been moving his ears slowly to and fro, flicking them and tossing his great head from side to side as if he were trying to shake something off.

"Why do you keep moving your ears?" asked the lion, forgetting his own problems for a moment.

"Can't you see it?" asked the elephant. "There's a gnat buzzing around my head. If he once gets into my ear that's the end of me."

The lion began to laugh. "Oh dear," he spluttered, "I don't mean to be rude, but here am I moaning because I am afraid of a cock. At least it is bigger than a gnat! I suppose everyone has something they are afraid of, but at least mine is not quite so shameful as yours."

## The Fox and the Grapes

ONE day a hungry fox went into a vineyard looking for food. The grapes were heavy and ripe, hanging in beautiful purple clusters on the vines, but they had been trained high on a trellis and though the fox strained and jumped he could not reach even the lowest branches.

At last, quite tired out, he turned crossly away muttering tetchily: "Who wants grapes like those, anyway. Anyone can see they are as sour as green lemons."

*Some people pretend to despise the things they cannot have.*

## The Bees and the Wasp

SOME bees once built a fine honeycomb in a hollow tree-trunk. Now there are two kinds of bees in a hive: worker bees, who spend their lives gathering pollen and making honey, and drones, who lie lazily in the hive all day doing nothing.

It happened that the drones began to boast that they had made the fine honeycomb. This made the worker bees very angry and they called a wasp in to decide who was right.

"It is very difficult to say which of you really built the comb," said the wasp thoughtfully. "You all look so much alike. However, I have a plan. I suggest that you each move into a different hive and each build up a new comb. When they are finished I will inspect them. From the shape of the cells and the taste of the honey I will soon know who built the fine honeycomb in this hollow tree."

"That's not fair," said the drones. "We don't want to build another comb. We are talking about the comb in this hollow tree, not some new comb."

"We'll start straight away," said the workers. "For we know we can do it."

The wasp turned to the workers.

"Now I know who can make honeycombs and who cannot. There is no doubt that the honey in the hollow tree belongs to you, workers."

*Actions speak louder than words.*

## The House Dog and the Wolf

A LEAN, hungry wolf met one moonshiny night with a plump, well-fed house dog.

"How is it that you look so sleek?" said the wolf. "Your food obviously agrees with you, while I can hardly keep myself from starving however hard I try."

"Well, if you want to eat as I do, you have only to do my job," said the dog.

"What is that?" asked the wolf eagerly, thinking of marrow bones.

"Just guard my master's house and keep the thieves away at night."

"When can I start?" asked the wolf. "I've had enough of living in the woods in all weathers. I wouldn't mind exchanging it for a warm roof over my head and a plateful of food whenever I need it."

"Follow me, then," said the dog and they trotted off towards the house.

As they were going along the wolf noticed a mark on the dog's neck.

"What is that on your neck?" he asked curiously. "There's a patch of your fur quite rubbed away."

"It's nothing," said the dog sharply.

"No, but tell me," said the wolf.

"It's nothing, I told you," said the dog. "It's probably just the collar my chain is fastened to. It rubs a bit sometimes."

"Chain?" cried the wolf in surprise. "Do you mean that you are not free to come and go as you please?"

"Perhaps not exactly as I please," said the dog. "You see they think I am rather fierce so they tie me up during the day. But of course at night I am quite free. Besides, the master feeds me from his own plate, and the servants all give me scraps and I am such a favourite and – what is the matter? Where are you going?"

"I'm off to the woods," said the wolf over his shoulder. "You can keep your dainty food and your warm roof. I'd rather have a dry crust and be free than have all the marrow bones in the world on the end of a chain."

*Freedom is more important than comfort.*

25

# The Trumpeter

LONG ago, when armies went into battle they took a trumpeter with them. He did not fight himself but he was very useful to the soldiers. Each tune he played on his trumpet meant something different. One tune told the soldiers to wake up in the morning, another tune told them to go to bed at night. One tune told them that the enemy was coming, another that they should stop fighting and return to camp. One of the most important things the trumpeter had to do was to play loud, angry music to make the soldiers fight more fiercely.

One day during a battle a young trumpeter was taken prisoner by two soldiers.

"Please don't kill me," he begged. "I am only a trumpeter, as you can see. I have not harmed a single one of your soldiers. Look, I am not even carrying a sword or a dagger – the only thing I have is this trumpet."

"That is exactly why you must die," replied the soldier, raising his sword. "For though you do not kill yourself you are just as dangerous. You give others the courage to fight."

*It is as bad to encourage violence as it is to commit it.*

## The Lion and the Bull

A HUNGRY lion sat watching a fat bull feeding in a field.

"If only bulls didn't have horns," thought the lion greedily. "Then I could soon finish him off. As it is he would toss me over the moon."

Then he had an idea. Sidling up to the bull he said in a friendly voice:

"I was just admiring you, Mr Bull. I hope you don't mind. What a handsome head you have. What big, strong shoulders. What powerful legs and hooves. If I may say so, though, I don't see why you put up with those horns. They must give you quite a headache and they do spoil your appearance you know."

"Do you think so?" said the bull. "I never thought about it. But now you mention it they do rather get in the way. Spoil my appearance did you say? Hmm."

The lion slunk away and hid behind a tree to watch. The bull waited until he was out of sight, then began to hit his head violently against a rock. First one horn splintered, then the other until soon the bull's head was smooth and bare.

"Aha," cried the lion, leaping out with a snarl. "I've got you now. Thank you so much for getting rid of your horns. They were the only things that prevented me from attacking you before."

*Don't listen to flatterers.*

## The Fox and the Stork

A FOX invited a long-beaked stork to have dinner with him.

"I hope you don't mind sharing the same dish with me," said the fox. "It is our custom in the wood to eat together to show that we are friendly."

"Not at all," said the stork politely.

The fox brought a wide, shallow bowl of thin soup and set it between them.

"Please help yourself," he said, settling down to lap the soup with his long pink tongue.

The stork stood with her long legs apart and put the tip of her long, thin beak into the soup; but although she tried to scoop up the thin liquid it was quite impossible for her to do so. Even when she did manage to hold a few drops in her beak they were lost long before they could trickle down to her throat. Too polite to complain, the stork went home hungry while the greedy fox lapped up all the soup. As she left she heard him laughing to himself at his own cleverness.

A few days later the stork invited the fox to have dinner with her in return and the fox made his way to her home.

"It is our custom to share a dish, too," said the stork. "I hope you will join me."

"Certainly, certainly," said the fox, licking his lips. He had not eaten all day.

The stork brought her food. This time, however, it was served in a tall, thin jug with a narrow opening at the top.

"Please begin," said the stork, thrusting her beak into the jug. "Mmmm. It *is* good."

Of course the fox could not get his nose into the jug at all. All he could do was sniff hungrily at the delicious smell and lick the occasional drop that spilled over the side.

"I suppose I can't complain," he said to himself sadly as he made his way back to the woods. "After all, I taught her the trick myself."

*Treat other people as you hope they will treat you.*

## The Oak and the Reed

THERE was a terrible storm one night in the forest. Many trees were blown down and branches were scattered far and wide. An oak tree that had grown by the side of a river was swept into the flood and carried downstream.

As the oak tree floated along it noticed to its surprise that the banks were still covered with reeds.

"However did you manage to survive?" it asked. "You look so thin and frail yet I, a great tree, lie dying."

"It is not surprising," whispered the reeds. "You were destroyed because you fought against the storm. We were saved because we gave way to it, bending to its slightest breath."

## The Boy and the Nettle

A BOY was playing in the fields when he was stung by a nettle. He ran home to tell his mother what had happened.

"I only touched it lightly," he said, "and the nasty thing stung me."

"It stung you *because* you only touched it lightly," his mother told him. "Next time you touch a nettle grasp it as tightly as you can. Then it won't sting you at all."

*Face danger boldly.*

## The Fox and the Lion

THE first time the fox saw a lion he fell down at its feet, ready to die of fright. The second time he still shook with fear, but he managed to raise his eyes and take a quick look at the lion's face. The third time he was so bold that he walked right up to the lion and began to talk to it as if he had known it all his life.

*Familiarity breeds contempt.*

# The Sick Lion

AN old lion lay ill in his den. All the animals came to visit him, but none of them could do anything for him and every day he grew weaker and weaker.

"Have you noticed, my lord lion," said the wolf one day, "that the fox has not been to see you? You can tell he doesn't care at all what happens to you, however much he flatters you when you are well and strong."

The fox happened to pass by at that moment and, overhearing the wolf's words, he put his long, foxy nose round the corner.

"I'm afraid, sire, that the wolf does not understand things too well. I care more about you than anyone. While he has been chattering at your side, I've been rushing all over the place trying to find a cure for you. I'm quite worn out."

"Have you found anything?" asked the lion eagerly.

"Yes, indeed I have. I found an old doctor who really knows what he is talking about. He says you must wrap yourself in the skin of a newly-killed wolf. That's the only thing that will make you better."

Before the wolf knew what was happening, the lion had sprung up and killed him for his warm skin.

"Aha!" laughed the fox. "You won't stir up trouble again in a hurry, Mr Wolf."

*Troublemakers make trouble for themselves.*

## The Donkey's Shadow

ONE hot summer day a young man hired a donkey to take him from one town to another. He rode along on the donkey's back while its driver walked beside them.

At midday the sun was so hot that the young man suggested they should have a rest. The driver led the donkey to the side of the road and the man dismounted. There were no trees to shelter under so he sat down in the donkey's shadow.

"Hey," said the driver, "that's my shadow. Move over."

The young man sat still.

"I've hired the donkey for the whole day, haven't I?" he asked.

"You may have hired the donkey but you certainly haven't hired his shadow as well," replied the driver, pushing at the young man's shoulder. "Move over and let me sit in *my* donkey's shadow."

The young man did not like being pushed one little bit and he pushed the driver back. They began to fight, punching and struggling to sit in the small patch of shadow.

They were so busy fighting that they did not even notice when the small patch of shadow moved quietly away.

"Fight over your own shadows," brayed the donkey as he disappeared smartly round a bend in the road. "I'm taking mine to a quieter place."

## The Stag and the Hedgehog

A STAG and a hedgehog once bought a field of wheat together, hoping to grow enough food to keep them through the winter. All went well until the wheat began to turn golden in the summer sun. Then, one day, they noticed that wild animals had broken through the hedge and were feeding in the field.

"We must guard the grain," said the hedgehog anxiously, "or there will be nothing left by harvest time."

The stag was chosen to keep watch. Very soon, however, the hedgehog saw that he was not doing his job properly. Instead of keeping other animals away, he joined them in trampling among the wheat, eating the ripest plants.

"This is no good," said the hedgehog. "I'll be the guard from now on."

Though the hedgehog was small he was so watchful, he sounded so cross and he looked so prickly that the other animals kept well out of his way and he managed to save most of the crop. Harvest time came. Then came the difficult matter of dividing the grain.

"I should have the larger share," said the stag. "I am bigger than you are and I need more food."

"I did all the work," retorted the hedgehog. "And I have a growing family to feed. We should have half each."

The two animals just could not agree. On the third day of their argument the stag invited a friend of his, a wild boar, to act as judge.

"Will you agree to do what I say?" asked the boar.

"Yes," said the stag.

"Yes," said the hedgehog.

"Then you must run a race. The winner of the race will have the whole harvest. I think that's fair." The boar winked at the stag when the hedgehog was not looking.

"It's not fair, it's not fair," said the hedgehog. "How can I win a race against a stag?"

The hedgehog went home sadly, wondering how he could find enough food to keep his family through the winter.

"Whatever is the matter with you?" asked his wife as he sat down glumly. "We'll think of something," she said when she had heard the story. "We won't let that scheming stag have everything his own way. I think I have a plan. You and I look very alike, don't we? I'm sure the stag cannot tell us apart and the boar doesn't even know you have a wife. This is what we'll do. You start running with the stag at the beginning of the race and I'll stand near the finishing post. As soon as I see him coming I'll start running as fast as I can. I'll make sure I get over the line first. Then the wheat will all be ours. After the way he has treated you, he doesn't deserve a grain of it."

The stag and the boar never did discover how the slow little hedgehog managed to run so fast. But the hedgehog family had enough food in their larder that winter to feed themselves and all their hungry friends and relations too.

*You may have to fight people who cheat with their own weapons.*

## The Thief and the Dog

A THIEF came to rob a house which he knew was guarded by a fierce dog. He brought a bag of meat with him and when the dog began to bark he threw him a piece of steak.

"That will soon shut him up," thought the thief.

But the dog was too clever for him.

"I had my suspicions about you when I first saw you," he said to the thief. "Now that you are so excessively generous to me I know that you are up to no good. Be off before I tear you to pieces."

*Watch out when strangers are nice to you. They may want something for themselves.*

# The Country Girl and the Milk Pail

A COUNTRY girl was walking to market one day, carrying a pail of milk on her head. As she walked along she began to daydream.

"When I sell this milk I shall get enough money to buy some more eggs," she thought. "I can put them to hatch under the broody hen and I shall have at least a dozen chicks to sell at the market. They will be ready just at the right time, when poultry is really expensive to buy, so I'll have enough money to buy a new dress.

"I wonder what colour of dress I should buy," she thought. "Green, I think. That suits me best. With a big, deep frill at the hem. Oh I'll look so delicious that all the boys at the fair will want to dance with me.

"I'll have nothing to do with them, though," she said to herself. "I'll just toss my head and walk away, however much they plead with me."

She gave her head a disdainful toss at the thought.

Unfortunately she had quite forgotten that she was carrying a pail of milk on her head. Down fell the pail, spilling fresh, creamy milk all over the road.

"Oh my beautiful green dress," she wailed. "Oh my chickens! Oh my good fresh eggs! Oh my milk!"

It was too late. The milk had all trickled away among the stones. With nothing left to sell at the market the girl carried her empty bucket sadly home.

*Don't count your chickens until they are hatched.*

34

## The Lion and the Bull

A LION once saw a large, well-fed bull grazing among a herd of cows in a field.

"That bull would make a fine meal for me," thought the lion. "But he is always surrounded by cows. They would soon trample me to death if I attacked him."

The lion went back to his den to think about the problem. The next day he returned to the field and called the bull politely.

"Will you do me the honour of coming to dinner?" he asked.

"Certainly," said the bull, feeling rather flattered. "I shall come today."

That evening the bull left his herd of cows and made his way to the lion's cave. He arrived rather early and there was no sign of the lion. The bull decided to explore the cave. He went cautiously inside. In the kitchen everything looked ready for a good meal. There were pans on the stove and dishes of vegetables on the sideboard. A spit was turning slowly over a hot fire, with a pot of dripping standing ready. On the table was a row of gleaming knives which looked as though they had just been sharpened.

"There is something missing," thought the bull. "Let me see. There is hot water

and vegetables and sauces and fat and . . . MEAT," bellowed the bull. "Where is the meat?" Though he looked high and low he could see no sign of any meat. "I have a strong feeling that I am the meat for this meal," he said to himself and without waiting any longer he hurried out of the cave and did not stop until he was safely home again.

Next day the lion came once more to the meadow.

"You did not come," he said in a hurt voice. "I took such a lot of trouble, and it was all wasted. If only you could have seen all the preparations I made."

"I came," said the bull grimly, "and I saw the preparations. That's what made me leave in a hurry. You hoped *I* would be the best part of that meal, didn't you?"

*You will not catch anyone out if you let them know what you are planning.*

## The Wolf and the Goat

A GOAT was feeding one day high on a rocky crag when a hungry wolf happened to pass below. The wolf tried several times to get a foothold on the rock but it was much too steep for him to climb.

"I wish you would come down a bit lower, little goat," he said. "You quite frighten me up there. If you are not careful you will slip and fall. Besides, the grass up there cannot be very nourishing. Down here it is rich and sweet. You'll get a much better dinner down here."

"Forgive me if I don't take your advice," bleated the goat. "You will get a better dinner if I come down, but I am not so sure that I will."

With that he skipped even higher up the mountain while the wolf loped disappointedly away.

*If you are wise, you won't take any notice of advice given by your enemies.*

## The Nightingale

THERE was once a nightingale who lived in a cage. Every evening her owner used to hang the cage in the open window and as it began to get dark the bird would sing her beautiful song.

One night a bat landed on the ledge above the window.

"Why do you only sing at night?" he asked. "I have never heard you utter a sound in the daytime."

"I used to sing during the day," said the bird sadly. "In fact I was singing happily one morning when I was caught and locked up in this cage. I'm more careful now. I only sing when it is dark and people cannot see me."

"It is a bit late to be careful now, isn't it?" asked the bat. "The time to be careful was before you were caught, not after."

*It's easy to be wise after the event, but much safer to take care before it happens.*

## The Donkey in the Lion's Skin

A DONKEY once found a lion's skin. He dressed himself up in it and began to run about the village, frightening everyone he met. Men, women, animals, chickens all fled away as fast as they could.

"Hee-haw," laughed the donkey. "This is better than carrying loads of wood about. See how frightened they are. Hee-haw, hee-haw!"

"So that's who you are," said a fox who had been hiding behind a wall. "You'd better keep your mouth shut if you want to be a lion."

*If you are pretending to be something you are not, be careful: it's easy to give yourself away.*

## The Horse and the Groom

THERE was once a groom who spent hours every day brushing, currying and rubbing down the horse's coat. Every day he would plait and unplait its mane, brush out its tail and shine its hooves.

In spite of all this care, the horse's coat grew steadily duller. Its eyes sank in its head and hairs began to fall out of its tail. For every day the groom stole half the horse's ration of corn and sold it for his own profit.

"If you really wanted me to look well," said the horse at last, "you would give me a bit less grooming and a bit more corn. Then I'd soon improve."

*Dishonesty is hard to hide.*

# The Wolf, the Fox and the Ape

THE wolf and the fox were old enemies. They were always trying to outwit one another and they used all kinds of tricks to gain an advantage. One day the wolf accused the fox of stealing a joint of meat.

"He's lying," said the fox. "I didn't steal his meat."

"I saw him," said the wolf. "He ran off with my lunch."

The fox appealed to the other animals.

"How can you believe a shifty-eyed, creeping cur like that?" he asked angrily. "Everyone knows he is about as straightforward as a two-headed viper in a thunder-storm."

"Ha!" sneered the wolf. "If you're talking about honesty there are one or two stories I can tell about you, Mr Fox. What about those hens you invited to supper? What about the little rabbit you kindly offered to help on its way home? I suppose they are coming to speak for you, are they?"

"Certainly," replied the fox with dignity. "I'll call them if you call a number of fine, fleecy lambs I have seen you with from time to time."

So they went on. No one could tell who was speaking the truth and at last they asked an ape to judge between them. The ape was a wise old animal and he listened in silence as they made their long, self-righteous speeches. Finally he said:

"In my opinion, Mr Wolf, you never lost the joint of beef at all. And as for you, Mr Fox, I am quite sure that you ran off with it as he says you did. Since you both obviously tell lies all the time I cannot believe a word either of you says. Be off before I send you both to prison."

*No one believes a known liar.*

## The Town Mouse and the Country Mouse

ONCE upon a time the country mouse invited his cousin the town mouse to stay with him.

The country mouse lived alone under a hedge in the corner of a field. His straw-lined nest was dry and warm and he lived there simply and safely from one year to the next.

When the town mouse came to visit, the country mouse made a great fuss of him. He gave him the best straw to sleep on and fed him with all the choicest things in his larder. There were grains of wheat and barley, nuts, cheese rinds and even little withered red apples that he had managed to carry from the orchard.

The elegant town mouse did not seem to be impressed by all these good things. He looked as if he hardly liked to sit down and only nibbled disdainfully at the food the country mouse put before him. As the evening drew on he grew more and more restless until at last he said:

"My dear mouse, how can you bear this plain, dull life? Nothing ever happens here, does it? You should see the place I come from. There is always something going on there. The streets are full of people – and the food! You don't have to work your life away scrimping and saving and scavenging to find the next crust. Why, food is just lying round for the taking in my town. A mouse, you know, does not live for ever. Come with me and see life while you can."

The country mouse was impressed by the town mouse's words and after a little more persuasion he agreed to go with him.

It was dark when they arrived at the town mouse's home and as the doors and windows were closed they had to scuttle in through a hole in the wall. The town mouse led the way to the dining room. The country mouse gazed around in wonder. There were thick carpets on the floor and thick velvet curtains at the windows. In the middle of the room was a table, covered with a white cloth and with food of every kind. A great banquet had been held there earlier in the evening and nothing had been cleared away. Dishes of turkey and joints of beef lay side by side with bowls of trifle, jugs of cream and wedges of the best French cheese. Loaves of crusty bread and half-empty flagons of wine were scattered around.

The country mouse stood and stared.

"Come on, country child," cried the town mouse and in a moment they were both scrambling to the table top. The country mouse did not know where to begin, but the town mouse guided him easily around, bringing him all the best tit-bits and urging him to try more and more different dishes.

"Oh my," said the country mouse. "This is really. . . ." Before he could finish his sentence the door of the room burst open and a crowd of laughing, noisy people came tumbling in to finish off the feast.

The two mice jumped off the table in fright and hid themselves in the first corner they could reach. The country mouse was too terrified to look up. Even the self-confident town mouse was shivering with alarm. After what seemed like hours the room grew quiet again and the mice crept cautiously towards the table.

They had scarcely started to eat again when something even more frightening happened. A cat came creeping through the open door and darted towards the table. The two mice managed to run behind a cupboard just as she sprang up to pounce on them.

As soon as it was all quiet again the country mouse said: "I've had enough of this town to last me for the rest of my life. Good-bye, cousin. The food may be rich and plentiful but it is not for me. I would rather live my dull life in peace than run these risks for my dinner."

With that he ran out of the house as fast as he could, back to his comfortable country life.

*For some people a safe, dull life is better than a rich, dangerous one.*

## The Ant and the Grasshopper

ONE cold, frosty day in the middle of winter a colony of ants was busy drying out some grains of corn which had grown damp during the wet autumn weather. A grasshopper, half dead with cold and hunger, came up to one of the ants.

"Please give me a grain or two from your store of corn to save my life," he said faintly.

"We worked day and night to get this corn in. Why should I give it to you?" asked the ant crossly. "Whatever were you doing all last summer when you should have been gathering your food?"

"Oh I didn't have time for things like that," said the grasshopper. "I was far too busy singing to carry corn about."

The ant laughed unkindly. "In that case you can sing all winter as far as I am concerned," he said. And without another word he turned back to his work.

*Plan ahead. You can't rely on other people to look after you.*

## The Eagle and the Raven

AN EAGLE was trying to break open a nut in his beak when a raven landed on a branch beside him. The raven eyed the nut hopefully.

"You'll never break it like that," he said. "If I were you I would fly up in the sky as high as I could, then drop the nut onto the rocks. It's the only way you'll get at the kernel."

The eagle flew up into the air until he was just a speck in the blue sky, then let the nut fall down, down, down to the ground. The raven hopped quickly from his branch and seized the nut in his beak. By the time the eagle had found his way back to the right place, all that was left was a broken piece of shell.

*Not all advice is good advice.*

# The Miser

THERE was once a rich man who sold all his property. He made a great deal of money, for he had many beautiful and valuable things to sell, but instead of spending it or putting it safely in the bank he bought one great lump of gold and buried it deep in the ground.

Every day he went secretly to the hiding place, dug down a little way to make sure the gold was safe and then carefully covered it all up again.

One day a man who worked in the garden happened to see him from behind the hedge.

"That is very strange behaviour for a rich man," he said to himself. "He's not digging for potatoes, that's certain."

The next day the gardener watched again.

"It can only be treasure that is hidden there," he thought. "And hidden treasure is there for the finder."

As soon as it was dark the gardener took his spade and dug up the gold.

The next day the rich man came as usual to inspect his gold. To his horror the hole was empty – all his wealth was gone for ever. As he sat moaning by the empty hole a neighbour came by and asked what had happened.

"I would not worry a minute longer about it," he said as soon as he had found out what was wrong. "Here, take this stone. Bury it carefully in the same place and pretend that it is your lump of gold. For as you never intended to do anything with the gold anyway, a stone will do you just as much good."

*Don't value money for its own sake, but for what you can do with it.*

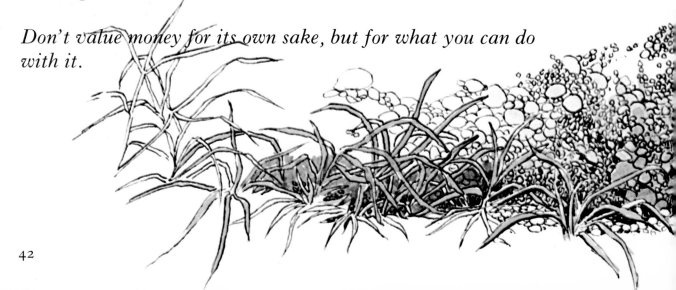

## The Fox and the Sick Lion

THE king of the beasts was ill. All day he lay curled up in his dark cave, sighing and groaning and giving faint, tired-sounding roars whenever anyone came near him.

The other animals did not know what to do. Usually the lion made all the decisions and now they were afraid of doing the wrong thing. At last, however, they agreed that the best thing to do was to visit him in his cave. If they stayed away he would certainly be angry, and he was obviously too ill to harm them even if he wanted to.

One by one, sometimes in small, humble groups, the animals made their way to the royal cave. Some took him presents – the best bit of meat they could find, or a bunch of fresh herbs. Others just went to talk politely about the weather. Large and small, they all made their way to the cave.

Only one stayed away: the fox.

After some time the lion noticed that the fox never visited him. He sent a jackal to look for him, to find out why he was being so rude.

"Fox," said the jackal, "His Majesty the lion is not at all pleased with you. There he is, lying dangerously ill in his cave and you have not even put your nose inside to ask how he is feeling. What excuse can you give for this disgraceful behaviour?"

"Jackal," replied the fox seriously, "it is not that I do not want to see the king. I respect him as much as anyone and several times I have come right to the cave mouth – with my best piece of chicken too."

"Well?" asked the jackal impatiently.

"Well, when I got there I noticed something that made me much too frightened to go any further, anxious though I was to see the king. I saw lots of footprints in the sand, footprints of many different kinds of animals. The strange thing was that they were all going one way – into the cave. There was no sign of any footprints coming out. That made me think very carefully, I can tell you."

The fox was right. The lion was not ill at all, but had thought of a way of saving himself a lot of trouble. Believing he was weak and harmless, the animals he usually had to hunt for food were all coming right into his cave – and ending up as his next meal.

"So you see I shall not be calling on His Majesty," said the fox.

*Think for yourself. What everyone else is doing may not be the right thing.*

## The Bat, the Bramble and the Seagull

A BAT, a bramble and a seagull once decided to go to sea together. The bat borrowed the money to buy the boat, the bramble packed a trunk full of fine clothes and the seagull took a pile of gold pieces.

After a time they ran into a storm. Their little boat was overturned and sank to the bottom. Though they managed to reach the land safely, they lost everything they had.

Ever since that time the seagull has flown low over the waves, diving down every now and then to see if she can catch a glimpse of the gold she has lost. The bramble tries to find her fine clothes: she clings fast to any she sees. The poor bat also lost everything. Now he only comes out at night because he is afraid of meeting the bankers who lent him the money to buy the boat.

*Some people allow one bad experience to affect their whole lives.*

## The Two Cocks

TWO cocks once fought to decide who should be king of the farmyard. After a long, hard struggle one cock could fight no more. He crept into the darkest corner of the henhouse to hide his shame.

The winner flew to the top of the farmhouse, crowing and flapping his wings to let the world know he was the new king.

"Look at me, look at me," he crowed. "I am the king of the farmyard."

Just then an eagle flew by. Swooping down, he seized the cock in his talons and carried him off.

The cock who was hiding in the henhouse heard the crows of triumph turn to cries of despair. He peered out to see what was happening. All at once he began to feel better. He fluffed up his battered feathers, straightened his drooping comb and strutted out into the yard again.

"I am king of the farmyard now," he crowed happily – just as if he had been the winner all along.

*Pride comes before a fall.*

## The Boys and the Frogs

A GANG of boys was playing at the edge of a pond when they saw some frogs swimming about among the weeds. They began to throw pebbles at them.

"Let's see how many we can hit," said one boy. "There, I got one."

"The first one to hit ten gets a prize," said another, picking up a heavy stone.

The frogs swam around in panic but one, braver than the rest, poked his head out of the water.

"Just stop and think a minute before you throw any more stones in here," he croaked. "It may seem like a game to you, but to us it is a matter of life and death."

*Always think how what you do affects other people.*

# The Mice in Council

ONCE upon a time the mice called a meeting to decide how they could get rid of a cat that was continually chasing them. She was a very clever cat. She could move stealthily, without a sound and when she pounced, she was as fast and as deadly as lightning.

Several mice put forward their ideas and the meeting went on far into the night. None of the plans seemed practical until at last a young mouse stood up.

"I suggest," he said, "that we hang a bell around the cat's neck. Every time she moves, the bell will ring and warn us. We shall hear her coming and be able to run away."

The other mice thought this was an excellent idea and there was a burst of excited and approving squeaking. Then an old mouse who had been sitting quietly all the time stood up.

"It is an excellent proposition," he said gravely, "and would, I am sure, be quite effective. But I have one question."

He paused.

"What is it? Ask your question," squeaked the other mice.

"Who," said the old mouse, "is going to *put* the bell around the cat's neck?"

This time, not one mouse had anything to say at all.

*It is often easier to have ideas than to carry them out.*

## The Wolf and the Donkey

A WOLF once met a donkey on the road outside the village.

"I'm going to eat you up," said the wolf.

"Certainly," replied the donkey, thinking fast. "But please don't eat me out here on the road where everyone can see. I shall be so ashamed. Take me into the forest. Don't be afraid that I shall try to escape. Here, tie this rope round your neck and fasten it to my bridle. Then I will lead you to a quiet spot I know."

The wolf thought this was a good idea so he fastened the rope round his neck and knotted it firmly to the donkey's bridle.

"Now I will go wherever you say," said the donkey.

"Show me the way to your quiet spot," ordered the wolf.

"Very well," said the donkey, setting off down the road towards the village. As they came to the first houses the wolf began to suspect that he had been tricked.

"This is not the way to the forest," he said, tugging at his end of the rope. "This road goes to the village."

"Don't worry," said the donkey cheerfully. "This is a short cut."

The donkey began to trot faster, then to gallop. The rope round the wolf's neck drew tight; in a very short time he was dragged right up to the donkey's door.

The master, his wife and their three sons all came running out to rescue the donkey. They were so angry that they would have killed the wolf there and then. Fortunately for the wolf, however, one of the sons threw a knife at him. The knife missed, but it cut the rope round his neck. The next moment all the family could see was a cloud of dust in the road as the wolf fled to safety in the dark forest.

*If you keep your head you will be all right.*

## The Fox and the Cicada

A CICADA was singing one evening in the branches of a tall tree when a fox happened to pass by.

"What beautiful singing," said the fox, peering up into the branches. "With a voice like that you must be a very handsome creature. Come down where I can admire your form as well as your voice." But to himself he said: "Aha, that's a cicada. He'll make me a tasty after-dinner snack."

The cicada had seen foxes before. Instead of hopping down himself he broke off a small leaf and sent it fluttering to the ground. The fox pounced on it greedily.

"You've given yourself away, fox," said the cicada happily. "I've never trusted you since I saw a pile of cicada wings outside your burrow one day. Now I know I was right about you. You can admire my voice if you like, but I'm not coming any closer."

*Don't trust flatterers. They usually want something for themselves.*

## The Tortoise and the Eagle

"IF ONLY I could fly," sighed the tortoise one day, looking up at the birds wheeling and gliding far above him. "What a different person I would be. It's just a question of getting off the ground. If I could get high enough in the air I could soar as well as any bird."

He began to practise little leaps, waving his forepaws in the air and stretching his neck as far as it would go. He even jumped off a couple of small rocks to try his skill, but each time he landed rather heavily on his stomach.

"If only I could get right up there where the wind would catch me," he grumbled.

One day when he was watching the birds as usual a great eagle landed on a low branch beside him and began to preen his feathers. The tortoise regarded him enviously. Then he had an idea.

"Will you teach me to fly, eagle?"

"Teach you to fly? Why that's impossible," laughed the eagle. "You have no wings for a start. You'd better stay on the ground, tortoise, where you belong!"

The tortoise did not give up. He pleaded and begged, offering the eagle all kinds of rewards until at last the eagle agreed reluctantly to help him.

"All you have to do is take me up into the air. Then I'll be carried along by the wind just as you are," said the tortoise confidently as the eagle grasped him in his talons.

Higher and higher the eagle rose until the trees and houses were matchstick toys below them.

"Now!" cried the tortoise excitedly. "Let me go and tell me what to do with my legs. . . ."

The eagle opened his claws but before he had time to give a word of advice the tortoise had fallen straight down to the hard, rocky ground far below!

*Don't try to be something you are not.*

## The Ant and the Dove

AN ANT once leaned too far over the edge of a fountain and fell into the water. A dove was watching from a tree nearby. She saw that the ant could not swim so she plucked off a leaf and threw it down to him. He just managed to scramble onto it and in time the wind blew him safely to the edge of the water.

As he crawled onto dry land again he saw a bird-catcher creeping stealthily towards the dove, holding a large net in his hand. Quickly the ant ran to where the man was standing. Just as he lifted the net to drop it on the unsuspecting dove, the ant bit him hard in the leg.

"Ouch!" said the man, dropping the net to rub his leg with his hand. "What was that?"

By the time he had picked up his net again the dove was flying safely to a better roosting place.

*One good turn deserves another.*

# The Fox and the Goat

ONE day a fox fell down a well and could not scramble out again. The water was not very deep but the sides of the well were smooth and covered in slippery moss so that every time the fox struggled up a few inches he slipped down again with a splash into the water.

After some time a goat came along and peered curiously over the edge.

"What are you doing down there, fox?" he asked.

The fox saw his chance to escape.

"Are you quite alone?" he asked mysteriously. "I don't want everyone to come at once. But the water in this well is so good that I just cannot stop drinking it. Come on in and try it. You'll see it is better than anything you ever tasted before."

Without thinking twice the goat jumped in and began to drink eagerly. After a while he had had enough to drink and he looked round to see how he could get out.

"No problem at all, my dear fellow," said the fox. "You stand on your hind legs and I'll climb on your back. If I balance on your horns I'll just about reach the ground. Then I'll lean over and pull you up after me."

So the goat stood on his hind legs and the fox climbed quickly out of the well. Trotting off across the fields he called out to the goat:

"If you had as much sense in your head as you have hairs in your beard, my friend, you would have made sure you could get out of that well before ever you jumped in."

*Look before you leap.*

## The Wolf who went Fishing

THE fox once overheard the wolf complaining about him to the other animals.

"He is always stealing things," said the wolf. "If I were you I would not trust him an inch."

The fox said nothing at the time, but he secretly resolved to get his revenge.

One day soon afterwards the wolf passed by the fox's lair. He paused to listen at the entrance.

"That was the best meal I have ever tasted," he heard the fox say. The wolf poked his head curiously inside.

"What did you say? Were you talking to me, fox?" he asked.

"Oh hello, wolf," said the fox. "I was just saying how good these fish tasted."

"Fish?" asked the wolf. "How did you get those?"

The fox's eyes glinted craftily.

"Come with me and I'll show you."

The two animals made their way to the edge of a pond.

"What you must do," said the fox, "is sit there with your tail in the water. The fish will come along to see what it is and when they take a nibble they will get caught up in the hairs. When it is heavy with fish you can pull it out and there's your dinner. That's how I do it, anyway."

The wolf thought this sounded much easier than running after rabbits and hares so he sat down on the bank as the fox had shown him and lowered his tail cautiously into the water.

"Brr, it's cold," he said. "But I suppose it's worth it."

"I'll leave you, then," said the fox, trotting off towards his lair. "Good luck. Be sure you wait until your tail feels heavy before you pull it out."

The wolf sat patiently waiting for several hours. At last, when it was quite dark, he decided to see what he had caught.

"My tail feels really heavy. I must have caught a lot of fish," he said to himself.

"Now, let's have a look what there is."

He stood up to pull his tail out of the water – then sat down again suddenly with a bump. While he had been fishing, the water in the pond had frozen hard and his tail was trapped fast in the ice.

"I'll kill that fox when I catch him," growled the wolf, beginning to shiver all over.

Just then he heard the sound of voices approaching and saw lights flashing across the fields.

"This way," he heard the fox bark. "The wolf is over here. I've got him well and truly trapped this time."

The fox had roused all the people of the village and they were coming with sticks and stones to beat the wolf.

"I'm not waiting for them," cried the wolf and with a mighty heave he threw himself forwards. There was an ominous cracking sound.

"Ouch!" cried the wolf. "My tail!"

He turned to look what had happened. Half of his thick, bushy tail was still in the ice. The part that was still attached to his body ended abruptly in a tuft of frosty hairs. Whimpering angrily, the wolf limped off to his lair.

"You've won this time, fox," he muttered. "But just wait till I get even with you!"

*Don't tell tales.*

## The Wolf and the Kid

A MOTHER goat went out to feed on the hillside, leaving her kid at home. She shut the door carefully.

"Bolt the door on the inside," she said to the kid, "and make sure you don't let anyone in. There's a nasty-looking wolf around the neighbourhood so keep the door tight shut until I come back. I'll knock three times like this when I am home so that you will know who it is."

Now it happened that the wolf was lurking just behind the hedge and he heard every word the mother goat said. When she had gone he waited for a short time, then crept up to the door.

Knock. Knock. Knock.

"Let me in, daughter. I am safely home from the hill," bleated the wolf, imitating the mother goat's voice. "Hurry up or the wolf will get me."

"You are back very soon," thought the kid. "I'll just make quite sure before I let you in." She stood on her hind legs to look out of the window. Sure enough, there was the wolf, standing by the door, trying to peep in through the letter-box.

"Be off with you," said the kid crossly. "You may sound like a goat but you look very like a wolf to me. Go and play your tricks on someone else."

*Better safe than sorry.*

## The Two Donkeys

A WILD donkey once met a tame donkey feeding on a hillside. The wild donkey was thin and small. He spent his life out of doors, sheltering as best he could in the cold weather and eating the sparse hill grass all the year round. He sometimes had to walk miles to find fresh water and at night there was always danger from prowling wolves.

The tame donkey was sleek and fat. During the summer he fed on the rich meadow grass but in winter he was given corn and hay to eat. There was always a pail of fresh water for him to drink and at night he was shut safely in a stable.

"How lucky you are," said the wild donkey. "I wish I could live like you."

A few days later the wild donkey was once more foraging on the hillside. Looking down he saw the tame donkey walking slowly along the road, carrying a heavy load of wood. As he watched, the tame donkey paused to snatch at a thistle growing by the roadside. Immediately his driver began to shout and to beat him with a stick.

"I've changed my mind about your way of life," thought the wild donkey. "I see that you have to pay heavily for the corn and hay they give you."

*It is better to be free and poor than to have everything you want and have to do what someone tells you all the time.*

## The Lioness

A FOX was boasting to a lioness.

"You should see my four pretty cubs," she said. "I had them all at once, you know. And what about you? How many cubs do you have?"

"I have only one," replied the lioness grimly. "But that one is a lion."

*It is quality that matters, not quantity.*

# The Travellers and the Bear

TWO friends were travelling along the road together when a bear came lumbering out of the forest in front of them. One of the men rushed for the nearest tree and, without a thought for his friend, climbed up to safety in the branches.

The other knew that he had no chance of fighting the bear alone so he threw himself on the ground and pretended to be dead. He had heard that bears never attacked a dead body so he lay as still as he could, holding his breath and hoping his heart-beats did not sound too loud. The bear snuffled and nuzzled at his nose and mouth, sniffed in his ear and poked greedily at his rucksack. Then he must have decided that the man was dead, for he lumbered off the way he had come.

For some time the traveller did not dare to look up. Then he cautiously raised his head and scrambled to his feet.

"You can come down now," he called to his friend.

Still trembling, the friend clambered to the ground.

"That bear put his mouth very close to your ear," said the friend. "What secrets did he tell you?"

"Nothing much," answered the other man. "He just told me to be careful not to choose friends who leave me in the lurch at the first sign of danger."

*When you are in trouble you find out who your real friends are.*

## The Old Woman and the Doctor

AN OLD woman who went suddenly blind called a doctor and promised him a large reward if he could make her see again.

"But if you fail," she said, "you will get nothing."

The doctor agreed that this was fair and they signed an official contract.

The doctor went to see the old woman every day. He soon discovered what was wrong with her eyes but he decided not to cure her straight away. Instead, each time he visited her he secretly took some of her things. At first he just took ornaments and jewels. Then he grew more greedy and began to carry off tables and chairs. At last he was so well organized that he arranged for a furniture remover to call and take everything away while he was upstairs with the old woman.

When he had taken everything he wanted he gave her some ointment which cured her blindness and sent her a large bill for his services.

Now when the old woman could see again she noticed at once that all her things had gone and she refused to pay the doctor's bill. He waited for several months but finally he took her to court to settle the matter once and for all.

The doctor explained his case to the judge. Then the old woman was called to tell her side of the story.

"What the doctor says is true," she said. "I did promise to pay him his fee if he made me see again and to give him nothing if he did not cure me. Now he says that I am cured – but I say I am not. Before I first went blind I could see all kinds of furniture, ornaments, china and jewellery in my house. But now when he says he has made my sight better again, I cannot see any of my things at all."

The old woman won her case and the doctor went angrily away without his fee.

*If you play tricks on people don't be surprised if they play tricks on you, too.*

## The Dog in the Manger

A DOG was once shut in a stable for the night with some horses. He looked around for somewhere comfortable to sleep and quickly settled down in the manger where the horses' food was kept.

When the horses came up to eat their evening meal the dog sprang to his feet, snarling and snapping his teeth angrily so that they could not come near.

"What a selfish animal you are," said the horses. "You cannot eat hay yourself and yet you will not let anyone else have a bite of it."

*If you can't make use of something yourself, give it to someone who can.*

## The Bundle of Sticks

A MAN once had four sons who never stopped quarrelling with one another. He was always telling them how much easier life would be if they worked together but they took absolutely no notice of him. One day he decided to show them what he meant.

He called all the sons together and put a tightly tied bundle of sticks on the floor in front of them.

"Can you break that?" he asked the youngest son. The boy put his knee on the bundle but though he pressed and pulled with his arms he could not bend the wood. The father asked each son in turn to try to break the bundle, but none of them could do it.

Then he untied the string and scattered the sticks.

"Now try," he said. The boys broke the sticks easily in their hands.

"Do you see what I mean?" asked the father. "If only you stand together no one can hurt you. If you all disagree the whole time and insist on going your separate ways, the first enemy you meet will be able to destroy you."

*United we stand : divided we fall.*

## The Olive Tree and the Fig Tree

AN OLIVE tree and a fig tree were talking one winter day.

"I feel sorry for you," said the olive tree. "Every year you lose all your leaves and have to shiver through the winter with bare branches. But I stay green and beautiful all the year round. Still, I suppose we can't all be good-looking."

The fig tree was silent. Later that day the weather turned very cold. Great grey clouds filled the sky and it was very still. It began to snow heavily.

All that night it snowed, and all the next day. Fields and hedges were thickly covered and people had to dig paths from their houses to the roadside. The snow settled on the olive tree, drifting in little piles on the leaves, weighing down the branches so that they snapped and fell to the white ground below. The fig tree was more fortunate. She had no leaves to trap the snow and it drifted harmlessly through the bare twigs.

When the thaw came she was still standing, ready to put out her new spring leaves; but the olive tree lay broken, a twisted jumble of sticks and brown leaves.

*Pride comes before a fall.*

## The Mountain

LONG ago a great mountain began to rumble and shake. People came from far and near to see what would happen.

"A great river will be born," said one.

"Surely nothing less than a mighty dragon will come out," said another.

"A god himself will spring from these rocks," said a third.

Finally, after days of expectation a small crack appeared in the mountain-side. And out popped – a mouse.

*Just because someone makes a lot of fuss, it doesn't mean he is important.*

# The Donkey, the Cock and the Lion

A DONKEY and a cock once lived together in a farmyard. One day a hungry lion came past. He noticed the sleek, well-fed donkey standing in the yard and he decided to eat him for his supper.

Now it is said that there is only one thing that lions are really afraid of – the crowing of a cock. And just as the lion was about to jump on the donkey's back the little cock began to crow at the top of his voice. At once the lion turned round and, with a roar of terror, ran as fast as he could out of the farmyard.

When the donkey realized that the great king of all beasts was frightened of a little farmyard cock he began to feel very brave himself. He chased after the lion, shouting and sneering as he went:

"A lion afraid of a bird! A lion afraid of a bird!"

They had not gone very far, however, when the lion's courage returned. Wheeling sharply round he grabbed the donkey at full gallop – and ate him for his supper after all.

*Don't take advantage of people's moments of weakness.*

## The Moon and her Mother

THE moon once asked her mother to make her a cloak.

"I want one that is a really good fit," she said.

"How can I possibly make a cloak to fit you?" asked her mother. "One day you are new, then you are full, and in between I don't know how many shapes and sizes. It is quite impossible. You are never the same shape from one night to the next."

## The Wild Boar and the Fox

A WILD boar was sharpening his tusks against a tree one day when a fox came by.

"What are you doing that for?" asked the fox. "There are no hunters around. Everything looks very peaceful to me."

"Quite true," said the boar, "but when the hunter does come with his dogs I shall be too busy running away to have time for this. So let me sharpen my tusks while I can."

*Be prepared.*

## The Fox and the Cockerel

A FOX was prowling round a farmyard one day when he saw a cockerel standing on a grassy mound.

"I've never seen such a handsome bird as you," said the fox. "Except for your father, of course. I used to know him well. What a voice he had. I don't suppose we'll ever hear anything like that again."

The cockerel preened his feathers.

"People say I have quite a good voice," he said modestly. "Perhaps you would like to hear it and see if it is as good as my father's was."

"Yes please," said the fox, turning away to lick his lips.

The cockerel stretched himself to his full height, closed his eyes tight and began to crow at the top of his voice. At once the fox grabbed him by the neck and ran off with him into the fields.

"Stop, thief!" shouted some men who were working there. "Give us back that cockerel." The men began to run after the fox.

"If I were you," said the cockerel, twisting his head round to talk to the fox, "I would tell them to mind their own business. Tell them I belong to you and they will stop chasing you."

The fox opened his mouth to call out – and the cockerel flew as fast as he could to the top of the tallest tree in sight.

"Why couldn't I keep my mouth shut?" the fox asked himself angrily.

"That was a lucky escape," thought the cockerel. "I'll keep my eyes open in future."

*Think before you act.*

## The Old Man and the Donkey

AN OLD man took his donkey to graze in a meadow and sat down on the grass to keep watch. Suddenly he saw a band of outlaws riding down the hill towards them.

"Run, donkey, run," cried the old man. "The robbers will take you."

The donkey looked up mildly.

"Do you think they will make me carry two loads at a time?" he asked.

"No, I don't suppose so," said the old man.

"Well then, I don't really mind if they do take me. I shall probably live just the same kind of life with them as I do with you. It doesn't make any difference to me whose loads I carry."

And he went on nibbling peacefully.

*Most people only care about changes when they are directly affected by them.*

## The Crab and her Mother

"WALK straight," said a mother crab to her daughter. "Stop dragging yourself sideways all the time."

"Mother," replied the daughter, "just show me how. If you walk straight yourself I will copy you."

*Don't expect people to do things you would not do yourself.*

## The Man and his two Daughters

THERE was once a man who had two grown-up daughters. One was married to a gardener and the other to a potter. One day the man went to visit the daughter whose husband was a gardener. He found her standing in the front garden sprinkling water on some young lettuce plants.

"How are you, my dear?" he asked.

"We are fine, thank you," she replied. "There's only one thing worrying us at the moment. This dry weather has gone on far too long. We need some good heavy rain for the garden. If it doesn't rain soon we shall be ruined."

Later the same afternoon the man called on the daughter who was married to a potter. She was sitting on the terrace of their little house, keeping watch over a long row of painted tiles that lay baking in the hot sun.

"How are you, my dear?" he asked.

"We are very well, thanks," said the daughter. "I just hope this fine weather will continue until our tiles are all hardened. Otherwise we shall be ruined."

The old man said nothing. Very soon he returned to his own house.

"Mind you don't pray for rain," he told his wife, "and be especially careful not to pray for fine weather. For whatever happens one of our children will be ruined."

*You can't please everyone.*

# The Boy who cried Wolf

THERE was once a shepherd boy who looked after sheep for all the people in the village where he lived. Every morning he collected the sheep from their owners and drove them out onto the hills to feed. Every evening he rounded them carefully up and brought them home again.

Some days it was pleasant on the hillside and the time passed quickly. On other days the boy grew bored and restless with nothing to do but watch the sheep nibbling at the short grass from morning till night.

One day he decided to amuse himself.

"Wolf! Wolf!" he shouted at the top of his voice. "A wolf is taking the sheep!"

The villagers all came rushing out of their houses to help him drive the wolf away – only to find the shepherd boy laughing till the tears rolled down his cheeks at the sight of their angry faces.

The boy tried the same trick again and again and each time the villagers rushed to his aid. Then, late one winter evening, just as the boy was thinking of gathering the sheep together to take them home, a real wolf came prowling around. The first the boy knew of it was a sound of frightened baaing from the sheep. Peering into the gloom he saw a long, grey shape creeping towards the flock.

The shepherd boy was very frightened. The wolf looked very big in the half darkness and he had only his crook to fight with. Shouting "Wolf! Wolf! A wolf is taking the sheep!" at the top of his voice, he raced towards the village. This time, however, the villagers did not come running out of their houses to fight the wolf. One or two of them looked up from what they were doing to grumble at the noise but most of them shrugged and said: "He has played that trick once too often."

Before the boy could find anyone to help him, the wolf had run off with all the sheep.

*No one believes a liar – even when he tells the truth.*

## The Fat Fox

A FOX discovered a store of bread and meat that some farmers had left in a hollow tree-trunk. He was feeling hungry so he squeezed himself through the narrow opening and gobbled it all up.

"That's better," he sighed happily as he wiped the last crumb away with his paw. "Now all I need is a good drink of water and I will be the happiest fox in the forest."

When he tried to wriggle out the way he had come, however, he stuck fast. He had eaten so greedily that his body had puffed right out. Only his head and one front paw hung out in the fresh air. The rest of him stayed inside the tree.

"The tree has got narrower," thought the fox. "Help! Help!" he called. "The tree is shrinking. I shall be squeezed to death."

Just then a thin weasel came past.

"What nonsense," he said. "The tree is the same size as it ever was. It's you that have eaten too much. There's no point my trying to pull you out. You will just have to sit there and wait until you get thinner again."

And that is just what the poor fox had to do for the next two days.

*Whatever you do, you must accept the consequences of your actions.*


## The Boy and the Lion

ONCE upon a time a shepherd boy was wandering far from home. He had lost his way in the forest and as darkness fell he felt very frightened and alone.

Suddenly a large lion came padding out of the trees towards him. The boy was just about to run for his life when, to his great surprise, the lion lay down, put his head meekly on his front paws and said:

"Don't be afraid. I will not hurt you. I have a thorn in my paw. See, it is deep in the pad and I cannot get it out."

The lion came closer to the boy and raised his paw.

"Goodness, that does look sore," cried the boy. "Come here and I'll soon get it out for you. It may hurt a little because I'll have to use my knife."

The boy sat down and the lion put his paw gently in his lap while the thorn was cut out.

"You'll be all right now," said the boy. "But try not to walk on it too much at first."

"Thank you," said the lion and without another word he disappeared into the forest.

Some time later the boy was falsely accused of stealing sheep. In those days the punishment for stealing was very severe: the judge ordered the boy to be thrown among a group of wild animals.

The boy stood bravely in the arena as the animals were let out, grasping the thick piece of wood he had been given to fight with. The biggest lion of all came bounding towards him. Then, to everyone's surprise, it sat down in the sand, raised its paw and bowed its head.

"Don't you recognize me?" asked the lion. "You helped me once in the forest when my paw was hurt. See, it is quite healed now."

The boy stood holding the lion's paw in amazement. The other wild animals soon backed away, seeing that the strongest of them all was refusing to fight.

"Let him go free!" shouted the crowd. "Give him a free pardon!"

"Come here, shepherd boy," commanded the king, who was watching from a special seat in the crowd. "You and your lion shall both go free."

From that time on the lion and the shepherd boy were never parted but lived as friends for the rest of their lives.

*One good turn deserves another.*

## The Frog and the Ox

AN OX who was feeding in a swampy meadow once trod on a family of frogs. Many of them were crushed but one escaped and hopped back to tell his mother what had happened.

"Mother," he cried, "there was such an enormous animal in the field. I have never seen anything like it."

The mother frog puffed her wrinkled skin out.

"Was it as big as this?" she asked.

"Oh much bigger, mother," said the young frog.

The mother frog puffed herself out even more.

"Was it as big as this, then?" she asked in a strangled-sounding voice.

"A hundred times bigger, mother. Even if you burst yourself with breath you would never reach half its size."

The mother frog was angry at the thought of someone being bigger than she was. Bending her thin froggy legs to the ground she took an enormous breath, puffing herself out and out until her wrinkled skin was as smooth as a drum and her eyes bulged with the effort.

"Big, bigger, big, bigger," she thought to herself. "Bigger and bigger and bigger and bigger. Biggest!" Until with a great gulp of air she burst with a bang and fell flat on the grass.

*Don't try to look bigger and better than you really are.*

## The Fox and the Mask

A FOX once found his way into an actor's house. He looked into everything. He sniffed at the costumes hanging in rows in the cupboards. He dipped his nose in the jars of cream and paint on the dressing table and he turned out the trunks full of pointed shoes and hats with plumes and feathers. Lying at the bottom of one of the trunks he found a perfectly made actor's mask. It had a nose, a mouth, eyebrows and even eyelashes. The skin was carefully coloured to look like real skin.

For a moment the fox thought it was a real face. Then, chuckling at his mistake he said:

"What a fine looking head you are. It's a pity you have no brains behind you."

*Beauty is no use without brains.*

65

# The Dog and the Bone

A DOG once stole a bone from a butcher's shop. He ran off down the street as fast as he could, across the village green and down the hill to a rough bridge over a stream. There he paused, panting, to look at the clear, clean water.

He gave a start. Looking up at him from the water was another dog. The other dog was holding a big, juicy bone in its mouth. The first dog glared at the second dog and the second dog glared fiercely back at him.

The first dog's mouth began to water.

"If I had that bone," he thought greedily, "I could eat it now and save mine for later. I know just the place to bury it. Besides, that bone looks better than mine. It has more meat on it."

The first dog growled threateningly – and the dog in the water bared its teeth and seemed to growl back at him.

"So you want a fight, do you?" growled the first dog, and he opened his mouth to grab the second dog's bone.

Splash! The first dog's bone fell into the stream and was swept away by the current. Barking angrily, he leaned forward to attack, but as his bone fell into the water the second dog seemed to vanish away. Its bone vanished with it. As the ripples gradually smoothed away the dog was left feeling rather foolish – and very hungry – staring at his own reflection.

*Be satisfied with what you have.*

## The Mouse

THERE was once a mouse who wanted to get married. She was a very proud mouse, and she did not want to marry just anyone.

"I'll only marry the strongest creature in the world," she said.

"What's that?" asked the other mice. She thought and thought.

"I'll marry the wind," she said at last. "He breaks down the tallest trees and he can even blow houses and castles down. He is the strongest creature in the world."

The mouse sent messengers to ask the wind to be her husband.

"Why does she want to marry me?" asked the wind.

"Because you are the strongest creature in the world," replied the messengers.

"Oh, but I'm not," said the wind. "There is a tower in the forest that has stood for more than a thousand years against my force. When I try to blow it down it just laughs and scatters my strongest gusts like draughts under a door."

The messengers told the mouse what the wind had said.

"Then I will marry the tower," said the mouse. "Go and tell him."

"Why does she want to marry me?" asked the tower when the messengers had spoken to him.

"Because you are the strongest creature in the world," said the messengers. "You are stronger than the wind."

"I am certainly stronger than the wind, said the tower, but I am still not the strongest creature in the world. Even I am gradually falling into ruin. Look around you and you will see who is stronger than I."

The messengers looked. All over the tower were little holes and crevices. The wood of its floors was gnawed and chipped and they could see the marks of tiny teeth on the walls. Even the mortar between its great stones was crumbling away.

"Can't you guess who has done this to me?" said the tower. "It is mice. Let your mistress marry one of her own kind: they are the strongest creatures in the end."

## The Wolf and his Shadow

THIS is the story of a wolf and his shadow. Have you ever noticed *your* shadow? In the morning when you get up it is on one side of you. Then it seems to shrink away until it is right under your feet and in the evening it stretches out longer and longer as the sun goes down.

It happened that one evening a wolf was walking by himself in a flat, lonely part of the country. The sun was very low in the sky and the wolf's shadow seemed to grow taller and taller every moment. The wolf looked at it in surprise.

"Is that really me?" he thought. "I had no idea I was as big as that. I must be at least a hundred feet long. To think that yesterday I ran away from a lion. If I am as big as this I should be king of the beasts myself."

The wolf strutted along proudly, feeling very big and strong. Soon the sun went down and the night animals began to stir themselves. He could hear roars and rustles around him but he went boldly on, confident that no one would attack him.

He was still telling himself how big and strong he was when a hungry lion leaped on him.

"You can't touch me, I am a hundred feet long," gasped the wolf.

"You look just like an ordinary wolf-sized wolf to me," said the lion as he gobbled him up.

*You may fool yourself into thinking you are more important than you are but you can't fool other people.*

68

## The Fox without a Tail

A FOX once escaped from a trap by biting off his tail and leaving it behind. At the time he was so relieved to be free again that he thought nothing of it, but as it healed he began to realize how odd he looked without it.

"I would almost rather be dead than look like this," he said. "Everyone will laugh at me."

Then he had an idea. He invited all the other foxes to come to an important meeting. When they were all sitting down, with their thick bushy tails curled comfortably round their paws, he began to speak.

"I expect you are wondering how I manage without my tail," he said to them. "The truth is that you just would not believe how much better I feel now than I did before. I can move more quickly, I never have to bother with getting brambles out of it all the time – and I don't get caught in traps. If I had not tried it for myself I would not have believed it either, but when you come to think of it a tail is just an ugly, inconvenient bit of extra weight. The wonder is that we foxes have put up with them for so long.

"Take my advice and have your tails cut off too. It could change your whole life."

When he had finished, an old fox stood up.

"I rather think," he said "that you would not be standing there telling us to get our tails cut off if there were any chance of you getting yours back again."

*If you can't have something, don't pretend you are better off without it.*

## The Fisherman

A FISHERMAN had been fishing all day without catching anything. As evening fell he found a very small fish on the end of his line.

"Please spare me," squeaked the little fish. "Please. I am too small to make you a good meal for I am not fully grown yet. Why don't you throw me back into the river. Then, when I am bigger and worth eating you can come back and catch me again."

"No, no," said the man, who was very hungry. "I am going to hold on to you now that I have caught you. If you once get back into the water you will take very good care not to come near me again and I shall have no supper now or later."

*Hold on to what you have.*

# The Soldier and his Horse

DURING the wars a soldier looked after his horse with the greatest care. He gave it the best oats to eat and the clearest water to drink. He rubbed it down when it got wet and covered it with a warm blanket on cold winter nights. As a result, the horse was strong and swift and carried its master safely out of the dangers of war.

When peace came, however, the soldier changed. He put the horse out in a field full of thistles and gave it only a little mouldy hay to eat. The stable was a broken-down hut with a leaking roof and a floor made of mud; the only water was in a ditch under the hedge. During the day the soldier made the horse work hard on his farm, carrying loads of wood and pulling heavy wagons.

After some time war broke out again. The soldier took out his heavy breastplate and boots, strapped on his pistols and helmet, and went to the field to catch his horse. Hastily brushing the thistles from its coat, he laid the leather saddle on its back, pulled the bridle over its mangy ears and heaved himself up.

For a moment the horse stood motionless. Then gradually its thin legs began to bend and it sank slowly to the ground. The horse gave the soldier a look of reproach.

"Master," it said, "you'll have to fight on foot this time. You have made me work like a mule and fed me like a goat. I cannot change back into a horse in an instant just because you want me to."

*Don't neglect old friends, even if you no longer need them.*

70

## The Old Hound

A HUNTER once had an old and faithful hound. For many years he had been the best dog in the pack, running more swiftly and catching more wild animals than all the others.

A day came, however, when he was really too old to carry on any more. After running half the day he managed to corner a wild boar in a clearing and to seize it firmly by the ear. The boar was young and strong and fought back well, shaking its heavy head from side to side as it lunged at the dog with its tusks. At last the old dog's teeth could hold on no longer and he was forced to let go.

The huntsman, following some way behind, came up angrily and began to beat the old dog with his stick as he lay on the ground panting wearily.

Looking reproachfully up, the dog said: "Master, don't beat me. I tried to fight but I was not strong enough. I have served you faithfully for a long time. Can you not remember what I was instead of punishing me for what I am now?"

*Respect the aged.*

## The Horse and the Stag

A VERY long time ago horses lived free all over the world. One of these horses used to feed every day in a grassy meadow. No other animal used the meadow and the horse felt that it belonged completely to him.

Then one day a stag came bounding over the hedge. He trampled carelessly all over the field, leaving deep footmarks and damaging the growing grass. The horse was very angry. He could not think of a way to get back at the stag himself so he asked the man who owned the field to help him.

"Of course I will help you," said the man. "If you just let me put this piece of metal in your mouth and let me sit up there on your back I will get my bow and shoot him for you."

The horse agreed and the man mounted on his back. But instead of riding off after the stag as he had promised, the man took the horse into his yard and set him to work. Ever since that time horses have obeyed man and worked as his slaves.

*Revenge is dangerous : it may hurt you as well as your enemy.*

## The Man and the Lion

A MAN and a lion were once travelling along together. As they went they began to argue about which of them was stronger and braver than the other.

They were beginning to get really angry with one another when they came to a statue by the roadside. The statue showed a man strangling a lion.

"There," said the man triumphantly. "What better proof can you want? One of our greatest artists cannot lie."

"That is just your side of the story," retorted the lion. "If we lions had artists I could show you plenty of pictures that showed lions strangling men."

## The Farmer and his Sons

AN OLD farmer called his sons to his bedside to read them his will.

"Children," he said, "the time has come for me to die. You will find all my treasure hidden in the vineyard."

As soon as the old man was dead the sons took their spades, their hoes and every tool they could find and began to dig in the vineyard to look for the treasure. They turned the soil over and over, digging deep into the rich, dark earth and breaking up the heavy lumps – just in case they concealed a bag of coins.

They found no treasure hidden in the earth but their thorough digging was so good for the vines that they yielded more grapes that year than ever before. The wine the brothers made was the best in the country and as everyone wanted to buy it, they made their fortune – just as their father had intended.

*You are much more likely to get rich from hard work than from a lucky win.*

## The Travellers and the Gold

TWO men were travelling along together when they saw a purse full of gold coins lying in the road.

"Look what I've found," said one, picking it up and putting it in his belt.

"Don't say 'I', say 'we'," said his friend. "We both saw it at the same time."

"I saw it first," said the first man.

After a while the man who had lost the purse came looking for it.

"Thief," he cried as soon as he saw it in the traveller's belt. "You have stolen my purse."

"What shall we do?" said the traveller. "It looks as if we are in a lot of trouble."

"Don't say 'we' are in trouble," said the second traveller. "You would not share the gold with me so I will not share the trouble with you."

## The Mole and his Mother

A YOUNG mole once boasted to his mother that he could see. Now the mother knew very well that all moles are blind: they live in dark underground burrows and do not need to see where they are going. She decided to find out whether the young mole was lying and she prepared a test. She laid a lump of sweet-smelling soap in front of him.

"Now, what do you see?" she asked.

The young mole touched the hard soap gently with his nose.

"A stone, mother," he said.

The mother laughed.

"You are not only blind like the rest of us," she said, "but you have no sense of smell either. If you had not boasted about being able to see I would never have found out about that."

*Don't tell lies. You'll only get caught out.*

# The Cock and the Ring

A FARMER'S wife once lost a diamond ring in the farmyard. She searched for it everywhere but as darkness fell she realized sadly that it was lost forever.

A few days later a cock was scratching among the stones when he saw something glittering in the sunlight. He pecked at it eagerly, thinking it might be some new kind of grain, but it was so hard that it almost shattered his beak.

"Well," he said to himself, burying it deep in the earth again, "you may be a fine stone to some people, I suppose, but you are no use to me. Give me a good grain of barley any day."

*People don't appreciate things they do not understand.*

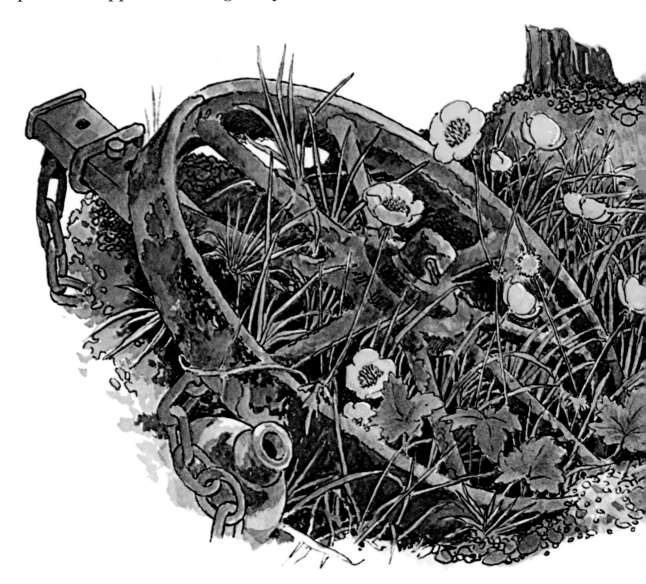

# The Fox and the Woodcutter

A FOX was being chased through a wood by a pack of hounds. As he ran panting into a clearing he found a man cutting logs of wood.

"Oh please hide me," said the fox. "The hounds are after me and they will tear me to pieces if they catch me."

"Hide here in the logs," said the woodcutter. "They will not find you here."

The fox ran gratefully under the pile of wood. Just then the hunters rode into the clearing.

"Have you seen a fox come this way?" they asked.

"Why no," said the woodcutter. But as he spoke he pointed towards the woodpile with his thumb to show the hunters where the fox was hiding. Fortunately for the fox the hunters did not notice and they rode on into the wood.

As soon as they were out of sight the fox crept out of the woodpile. He was stealing off without saying a word when the woodcutter said crossly:

"Aren't you going to thank me for saving your life, then?"

"No thanks to you," replied the fox. "I saw the whole thing from under those logs. You may have saved my life with your words, but you tried your best to give me away with your thumb. No, you'll get no thanks from me."

And he ran off into the woods.

*Actions speak louder than words.*

# The Wolf and the Lamb

A WOLF was drinking from a running stream one day when he saw a lamb paddling lower down.

"I'd like that lamb for my dinner," he thought. "But what will people say? I must have a good reason for killing her."

He thought for a moment. Then:

"You thoughtless creature," he shouted. "How dare you stir up my drinking water. You are making it all muddy with your silly feet."

"Excuse me, sir," said the lamb, "but I do not see how I can be doing that. The water flows from you to me, not from me to you. So what I do down here cannot possibly affect you up there."

"Never mind that," answered the wolf crossly. "I've had enough of your rudeness. It is only a year since you were so abominably impertinent to me before and here you are again answering back."

"Oh sir," cried the lamb, getting rather frightened. "I was not even born a year ago."

"What do I care when you were born?" said the wolf. "If it wasn't you it was your father. It's all the same to me. I won't be argued out of my dinner."

And without another word he pounced on the lamb and gobbled her up!

*There is no point arguing with a determined person. He will do what he wants anyway.*

## The Owl

ONE day when the birds were all together they found a very beautiful rose growing by itself on a small bush. Each bird wanted to have the rose for itself so they decided to give it as a prize to the most beautiful of them all.

One by one the birds of the world strutted and hopped before the judges. There were brightly-coloured parrots and parakeets, peacocks with their shimmering tails, tiny humming birds and long-plumed birds of paradise, snow-white doves and gleaming black ravens. It was very difficult to choose among so many.

Then an owl came hopping forward.

"Let me save you some trouble," he said. "It is easy to see that I am the most beautiful bird of all. Give me the rose."

The other birds all laughed.

"The only thing that is easy to see is that you are *not* the most beautiful bird of all," they said. "Go away, everyone. It is late. We will decide tomorrow."

During the night the owl crept up to the rose bush and stole the rose.

"If they won't give me the prize then I shall take it for myself," he said.

Next morning, when the other birds discovered what had happened, they were very angry.

"The owl must be punished," said the eagle.

"Since he stole our rose at night, he shall never fly in daylight again," said the thrush.

"He shall see by night but not by day," said the bullfinch.

"Since he thinks he is so much better than we are, he shall live apart from us," said the sparrow.

"So be it," said the eagle.

And that is why the owl is a solitary bird of the night; if the other birds ever find him flying in the daytime they swarm round him like angry bees, pecking and shrieking at him until he returns to the shelter of the dark woods.

## The Farmer and the Eagle

A FARMER once caught an eagle in a trap.

"I cannot let a magnificent bird like you end up in a cage," he said, releasing the spring that held the bird's leg. "You should be free to fly over the mountains and soar in the sky."

The bird looked at him gratefully and flew off. A few days later the farmer was resting at midday in the shade of an old wall. He was dozing comfortably after his lunch of bread and cheese when suddenly the eagle swooped down and plucked off his cap.

"What's that?" cried the farmer with a start, leaping to his feet and running after the bird. "Give me back my cap this minute. What kind of gratitude is that?"

The eagle flew several yards away, then dropped the cap and hopped about on the ground beside it. The farmer picked the cap up, dusted it down, then turned crossly away. He was just in time to see a large section of the wall where he had been sitting crumble and fall in a heap.

"Why, you saved my life, eagle," he said, looking round for the bird. But the eagle had flown away, and was only a speck in the clear blue sky.

*One good turn deserves another.*

# The Hare and the Tortoise

THE hare was always laughing at the tortoise because he walked so slowly.

"Really I don't know why you bother to go at all," she sneered. "By the time you get there it will all be over – whatever it is."

The tortoise laughed. "I may be slow," he said, "but I bet I can get to the end of the field before you can. If you want to race, I'll prove it to you."

Seeing an easy victory the hare agreed and she bounded off as fast as she could go. The tortoise plodded steadily after her.

Now it was the middle of a very hot sunny day and before long the hare began to feel a little drowsy.

"I think I'll just take a short nap under this hedge," she said to herself. "Even if tortoise passes by I'll catch him up in a flash."

The hare lay down in the shade and was soon fast asleep.

The tortoise plodded on under the midday sun.

Much later, the hare awoke. It was later than she had intended but she looked round confidently.

"No sign of old tortoise, I see, even if I did have rather more than forty winks."

Away she went, running through the short grass and the growing corn, leaping ditches and brambles with ease. In a very short time she turned the last corner and paused for a moment to look at the place where the race was to end. There, not a yard from the finishing line was the tortoise, plodding steadily on, one foot after another, nearer and nearer to the end of the race.

With a great bound the hare streaked forward. It was too late. Though she threw herself panting over the line, the tortoise was there before her.

"Now do you believe me?" asked the tortoise. But the hare was too out of breath to reply.

*Slow and steady wins the race.*

## The Young Man and the Cat

ONCE upon a time there was a sleek tabby cat. She lived in a small house in the town with a handsome young man. He was always very kind to her. He gave her milk to drink and pieces of fresh fish and meat to eat. He let her play in the garden during the day and at night she was allowed to come and go as she pleased, for he always left a little window by the back door open for her.

In return she kept the house clear of mice and rats, she sat on his knee in the evenings and she woke him up purring at the foot of his bed in the mornings.

The young man lived quite alone except for the cat. He had no mother or father, no brothers and sisters, and hardly any friends.

"You are my only companion," he used to say to the cat in the evenings as they sat by the fire. "Without you I should die of loneliness in this unfriendly town."

"I wish I could talk to him," thought the cat. "I wish I could tell him how much I love him. If only I were a human being I am sure I could make him love me too. Then he would never be lonely again."

All she could do, however, was purr and rub her soft nose affectionately against his sleeve.

Now it happened that Venus, the goddess of love, was looking down into the young man's house at that very moment, wondering what to do about him. She listened to the cat's secret thoughts.

"I wonder," she said to herself, "I wonder. Yes, I shall try it."

That night while the cat was out hunting in the garden, Venus cast a strong spell on her and changed her into a human being. In the morning when the young man opened the back door to see where his little cat had run to he found a beautiful young girl standing there.

The young man soon fell in love with the gentle girl he had found in his garden. He had never seen anyone quite like her. Her hair was all colours of brown and gold and her large eyes looked sometimes green and sometimes yellow. She had long, pointed fingers and toes and she moved so lightly and easily that she seemed to float over the ground. Strangely, she seemed to know her way around the town although he was sure he had never seen her there before. After a very short time they were married.

The young man and the girl were very happy together. During the day while he was at work she cleaned the house, cooked the dinner and mended his clothes. In the evenings they sat in front of the fire and talked about all the things they would do together. From time to time the young man would say:

"If only you had seen my funny little cat. Before you came, she was all I had. I know you would have loved her too."

The girl would smile to herself, remembering faintly that there had been other times that the man knew nothing about.

One evening, a year after their wedding, Venus looked down at them again.

"It looks successful," she said, "but I wonder if it will last. I think it is time I gave her a test."

Later that night, just as the girl and the young man were falling asleep, Venus set a small, frightened mouse down in the corner of their bedroom. It pattered round the skirting board for a minute, trying to find a hole to escape down. Then it gave a tiny squeak. At once the girl sat straight up in bed, her nose twitching, her eyes opening wide in the darkness. Then the mouse made a sudden dash across the carpet. The girl was out of bed in a flash. Her long fingers pounced on the mouse and she raised it eagerly to her mouth.

As the young man watched in horror

from the bed there was a small flash and a high-pitched hissing noise. When he could see properly again the girl had vanished. In her place stood a small tabby cat. The mouse had disappeared.

The little cat shook her head a little, as if she did not quite know what was happening to her. Then with one spring she was on the bed beside him, rubbing her nose against his chest.

"I don't know what happened," said the young man, "but I'm glad to see *you* back again, little cat."

*You can't change your own nature.*

## The Hares and the Frogs

THE hares were once so badly treated by everyone that they did not know what to do. Dogs chased them, men shot at them, even eagles and crows carried them off. The hares decided that life was just not worth living any more. The only thing to do was to kill themselves and get away from all their misery.

They made their way in a large group to a lake where they could drown themselves. As they ran up to the bank they frightened a family of frogs who were sitting there sunning themselves. The frogs leaped into the water in great alarm, jumping on top of one another in their haste to get away.

The first hare stopped suddenly.

"We are not as badly off as we think, you know," he said. "We think everyone is bigger and stronger than we are – but here is a whole crowd of creatures who are actually afraid of us. Come, let us try to be as brave and strong as they think we are."

*There is always someone worse off than you.*

## The Boy and the Nuts

A BOY once found a jar full of nuts and raisins in his mother's kitchen and he put his hand in to help himself to as many as he could hold. When he tried to take his hand out of the jar, however, he found that the opening was too narrow for his clenched fist to pass through.

"Whatever shall I do?" he wailed. "My hand will be stuck in this jar for ever."

Just then his mother came in.

"Really," she said, "there's nothing to make such a fuss about. Try taking half as many nuts and raisins as you have in your hand and you'll find it comes out of the jar quite easily."

*Don't be greedy.*

# The Thieves and the Cock

TWO thieves were prowling round a deserted farm one night looking for something to steal. They searched the house from cellar to attic but they could not find anything at all.

As they were leaving, one of the thieves fell over a young cockerel that was roosting with some hens on a low branch. The cockerel gave a loud squawk and started to run fluttering across the fields. The men followed him as fast as they could, tripping and stumbling. At last one of the men lunged forward and grabbed the cockerel by the leg.

"Got you!" he panted. "At least we'll have a good supper after this night's work."

"Please don't take me," the cockerel pleaded. "I am much too useful a bird to end up in the pot."

"What use are you, then?" asked the thief.

"Why, I wake people up at daybreak so that they can get to work on time," said the cock proudly. "I am a very useful bird indeed."

"All the more reason why we should kill you," said the thief, tucking the cockerel firmly under his arm. "If you wake people up so early how do you expect us to have time to do our stealing?"

*A cunning person will twist an argument to suit his own ends.*

82

## The Young Man and the Swallow

THERE was once a young man who was left a large fortune by his father. Instead of looking after it carefully he spent it as fast as he could until quite soon it was all gone.

The only things the young man had left were his thick winter clothes. He had a long coat made of fur, a pair of fur-lined leather boots and some fur-lined gloves. The winter had been very cold and the young man was glad that at least he had been able to keep himself warm.

One day in early spring he looked out of his attic window and saw a swallow darting under the eaves of the house.

"A swallow is a sure sign of summer," said the young man. "Now at last I can sell these heavy clothes and make some money for myself."

He ran out to the shops and sold his fur coat, his fur-lined leather boots and his warm fur-lined gloves. The furs were valuable and the shopkeeper gave him a lot of money for them. But the young man had not changed his ways. As soon as he had money in his pocket he went straight to the most expensive shops and spent it all. By evening he had nothing.

The next day the young man woke up early, shivering with cold. The weather had changed in the night. There had been a hard frost and now it was snowing. The young man had no warm clothes to protect him – only a thin shirt and a pair of worn trousers. He opened the window a crack to look out. There on the window-sill lay the swallow he had seen darting in the sunshine the day before, now half dead with cold.

"Poor thing," he said, lifting it care-fully in his hands. "I wish I had not seen you yesterday. You and I thought that summer had come to stay – and now look at us."

*One swallow does not make a summer.*
*Don't trust the first sign you see.*

## The Boy and the Wolf

A WOLF once found a boy hiding behind a haystack, trembling with fright.

"Please don't eat me," pleaded the boy.

"I don't see why I shouldn't," replied the wolf. "But if you can tell me three things that are really true, then I will let you go."

The boy thought for a moment. Then he said:

"First, I wish you had never seen me. Second, I was stupid to let you find me here and third, I hope the hunter gets you tomorrow to stop you stealing all my sheep."

"Fair enough," said the wolf, who was not feeling hungry anyway. "I am sure those are all true from your point of view. Now run off before I change my mind and gobble you up."

*It pays to tell the truth.*

## The Lion and his Advisers

THE lion called a sheep to him one day and said:

"Tell me the truth, sheep. Does my breath smell?"

"Yes," said the sheep.

"How dare you insult me!" roared the lion, and he bit off her head.

Next he called the wolf to him.

"Tell me the truth, wolf," he said. "Does my breath smell?"

"Certainly not," said the wolf.

"Flatterer!" roared the lion, and he bit off his head.

Finally he called the fox to him.

"Tell me the truth, fox," he said. "Does my breath smell?"

"I cannot tell you whether it does or not," said the fox cunningly. "I have a bad cold in my nose and have quite lost my sense of smell."

*Sometimes it is safer not to have an opinion.*

84

## The Crow and the Jug

ONE hot summer day a thirsty crow was looking for some water to drink. There had been no rain for several weeks and all the puddles and ponds he usually drank from were dried up into jigsaw patterns.

At last he saw a jug standing outside the back door of a house. He poked his head inside. He could smell the water, he could see the water, but he could not reach the water. The jug was tall and even when he put his head right in and jumped off the ground it was still too deep for him.

He stood on the step for a minute.

"Perhaps I could break the top of the jug off with my beak," he thought.

He tried. Nothing happened.

"Perhaps I could turn the jug on its side so that the water runs out," he thought.

He tried. Nothing happened.

"Ah," cawed the crow aloud. "I know what to do."

The path at the back of the house was covered in small pebbles. The crow hopped off the step and picked a pebble up in his beak. Then he hopped up and dropped the pebble into the jug. Back and forth he went, dropping pebble after pebble into the jug. Gradually the pebbles filled the bottom of the jug and pushed the water higher and higher. At last, after at least a hundred trips up and down the steps, the crow was able to dip his tired beak into cool water and drink his fill.

*Where there's a will there's a way.*

## The Farmer and the Snake

ONE snowy evening a farmer found a snake lying on the roadside, stiff as a stick, half dead with cold. He felt sorry for it and he picked it up, put it in his pocket and took it home to warm it by the fire.

After a little while the warmth of the flames began to revive the snake. It gave a wriggle, then a twist, then raised its head and looked around with its tongue flickering in and out.

The farmer's family crowded round to watch. Suddenly, without warning, the snake darted at the youngest child and bit her in the leg.

"Why do you repay my kindness with spite?" asked the farmer.

"You should know better than to trust me," replied the snake. "You and I are old enemies. Why should I forget just because you were soft-hearted?"

"I know better now," said the farmer angrily and with one blow of his stick he killed the snake stone dead.

*Don't expect gratitude from people who dislike you.*

## The Two Pots

TWO pots, one made of earthenware and one made of brass were floating down a river.

"Stay close to me," said the brass pot. "I am strong. I will look after you."

"It is kind of you to offer," replied the earthenware pot, "but that is just what I don't want to do. If you will only stay away from me I shall float along quite safely. But if I knock into you I shall break into little pieces."

*Be very careful when you deal with strong people. They may hurt you without meaning to.*

# The Kid on the Roof

A KID stood on a roof ridge chewing bits of old thatch when a prowling wolf passed by below, looking for a meal.

"Hello, wolf," said the kid. "You're looking very downcast this morning. Are you looking for a slug or a fat caterpillar you can gobble up with those big ugly teeth? They've fallen out, did you say? Then perhaps you can chase some old she-cat from her milk bowl."

The wolf looked up.

"Kid," he said mildly, "get on with your nibbling of old straws and be thankful that for once your giddy head is emptier than my belly. You talk bravely up there on the roof top but down on the ground you would soon learn to treat your betters with respect. Take care to keep out of my way when we are on the same level!"

*It is easy to sound brave when you are not in danger.*

86

## The Birds, the Beasts and the Bat

BATS are curious creatures. They have bodies like mice, but they can fly in the air like birds. Nowadays they always live in dark places and do not like coming out in the daylight at all, but once, long ago, things were different. This is how it happened.

There was once a fierce war between the birds and the four-footed animals. At first no one could tell who would win, for both sides seemed very strong. The bat, half bird, half beast, did not know who to fight for so he thought he would wait and see what happened. After a time the four-footed animals began to win and the bat decided to join with them. He was very useful to them because he could fly and was able to attack the birds in the air. Before long, however, the birds grew strong again.

"Oh dear," thought the bat, "I have chosen the losing side," and he quickly began fighting as hard as he could *against* the four-footed animals.

Eventually the birds were declared the winners. Peace was made and the leader of the birds and the leader of the four-footed animals met to talk over the battle.

"Your side fought bravely," said the eagle generously.

"But you were stronger," said the lion. "And of course you do have one advantage: you can fly."

"That reminds me," said the eagle thoughtfully. "Didn't I see one of your beasts flying among my birds and doing a lot of damage?"

"Oh him," said the lion in a disgusted voice. "He is no beast of mine. He is a bat. I notice he was fighting on your side at the end. I thought he must be a bird."

"Certainly not," said the eagle. "We do not have traitors in our army. If I ever see him again I will throw him right out of the animal kingdom."

"And I will help you do it," said the lion, baring his teeth in an angry snarl.

Ever since that time the bat has not dared to come out in the daylight. He waits until the birds and the four-footed animals are safely asleep before he shows his mousey face in the world.

*Don't try to take both sides in a quarrel.*

## The Wise Hare

IT HAD been a very bad year in the forest. Food was running short and the animals all met together to discuss how it should be shared out.

"I think every animal should have an equal share," said a hare bravely.

"You have made a good speech," said the lion, "but it would be more use to you if it had claws and teeth like ours."

*It is no use having good ideas if you are not strong enough to carry them out.*

## The Mouse and the Bull

A MOUSE once took a bite out of a bull's tail as he lay dozing. The bull jumped up in a rage and, with his head low to the ground, chased the mouse right across the yard. The mouse was too quick for him, however, and slipped easily into a hole in the wall.

The bull charged the wall furiously again and again, but although he bruised his head and chipped his horns, the mouse stayed safely inside his hole. After a time the bull gave up and sank down to rest again.

As soon as the bull was asleep, the little mouse crept to the mouth of the hole, pattered across the yard, bit the bull again – this time on the nose – and rushed back to safety. As the bull roared helplessly the mouse squeaked:

"It's not always the big people who come off best. Sometimes the small ones win, you know."

## The Lazy Donkey

A MAN bought a donkey at the market one day and took him home on approval. Now the man owned several donkeys already and he knew each one's character very well. One of the donkeys was very strong and brave. Another was eager to please but quickly exhausted. One donkey was very lazy. He hated going to work in the morning and he did as little as he possibly could all day long. When the other animals were being loaded up he always tried to be last so that he would get the lightest load.

The man led the new donkey into the stable yard. For a moment he stood sniffing at his new companions. Then, without hesitation, he trotted up to the lazy donkey and began feeding comfortably at his side.

Though it was late in the day, the man immediately led the new donkey out of the yard, straight back to the market.

"You cannot have given him a fair trial yet," said the merchant. "It is only ten minutes since you bought him."

"I don't need to try him any more," replied the man. "I know just what he is like from the friend he chose for himself. Take him away and give me my money back. I can do without donkeys like him."

*You can tell what people are like from the friends they choose.*

## The Wind and the Sun

THE wind and the sun were once arguing about which of them was the stronger. As they could not agree, they decided to arrange a contest.

"You see that traveller down there," said the wind. "Whichever of us makes him take off his cloak is the stronger. Do you agree?"

"That seems fair to me," said the sun. "You try first."

The wind began to blow with all his strength. Storm clouds raced across the sky and trees twisted in the icy gale. Leaves whirled all around and great branches cracked and splintered. As the wind blew more and more strongly, the traveller wrapped his cloak closely round him, gripping it tightly in his hands.

Then the sun appeared from behind one of the storm clouds. The cold air grew warm and soft and the traveller looked up, surprised at the sudden change in the weather. As the sun rose higher and higher in the sky his rays grew stronger until at midday the traveller could stand the heat no longer. Throwing off his heavy cloak he lay down in the shade of a tree to sleep.

"I think that proves who is strongest," said the sun. But the wind had crept away to hide.

*Kindness and gentleness are often more effective than force.*

# The Wolf in Sheep's Clothing

A WOLF once decided that if he disguised himself he would be able to get plenty to eat without being hunted and shot at wherever he went. So he wrapped himself up in a sheepskin and slipped in among a flock of sheep that was feeding nearby.

He stayed with them all day, pretending to nibble the grass as they did and when evening came he was locked up in the fold with them. He was just about to take one of the sheep for his supper when he heard footsteps coming towards him. The shepherd had also decided to have a sheep for his supper and, taking out his long knife, he killed the biggest one he could see.

You can imagine how surprised he was when he took off the fleecy wool and found a large, grey wolf lying dead inside. By chance the shepherd had chosen him from all the others. The wolf's disguise had been just a little too perfect!

*Pretending to be something you are not may get you into trouble.*

## The Frogs and their King

ONCE upon a time the frogs decided to ask Jupiter, the king of the gods, for a king of their own. Jupiter was amused.

"Here you are," he said, throwing a log of wood with a splash into the lake where they lived. "Here is a king for you."

The frogs dived under the water in fright, burrowing as deep into the mud as they could. After a time one of the braver ones swam cautiously to the surface to take a look at the new king.

"He looks very quiet," said the frog. "Perhaps he is asleep."

The log stayed quite still on the smooth lake and one by one more frogs came up to take a look. They swam closer and closer until at last they leaped right on top of it, quite forgetting that they had ever been frightened. Young frogs began to use it as a diving board; old frogs sat sunning themselves on it; mother frogs taught their tadpoles their first, wobbly jumps on its bark.

One day an old frog said: "This is a dull kind of a king, you know. I thought we wanted someone to keep us in order. This one just lies around and lets us do what we please."

So the frogs went once more to Jupiter.

"Can't you give us a better king?" they asked. "Someone who will be a bit more active than the one you sent before?"

Jupiter was not in a good mood.

"Silly little animals," he thought. "I shall give them just what they deserve this time."

He sent a long-legged stork to the lake.

The frogs were very impressed and crowded admiringly round. But before they could even begin the speeches of welcome they had prepared, the stork stuck his long beak into the water and began to gobble up as many frogs as he could see.

"That's not what we meant at all," gasped the frogs as they dived once more into the mud. But this time Jupiter would not listen.

"I only gave you what you asked for," he said. "Perhaps it will teach you not to complain about things so much."

*Be content with what you have.*

## The Wolf and the Child

A WOLF was sniffing round outside a house looking for food. As he passed under a window he heard a child crying and its mother scolding it.

"Stop crying this minute," said the mother crossly. "If you don't stop I'll throw you out of the window and the wolf will get you."

The wolf grinned to himself.

"If I wait around here for a while I shall get a fine supper," he thought. So he lingered round the house hopefully, listening to the child's cries.

As evening came on and it began to grow dark the child began to cry again and the wolf crept nearer to the window. Again the mother was talking, but this time her voice was soft and kind.

"Don't cry, baby," she said. "Don't cry. The nasty wolf shan't have you."

Hungry and disappointed the wolf slunk back to the woods muttering: "That's what comes of believing people who say one thing and mean another."

*Don't believe everything you hear.*